A Retreat with Thomas Merton

A Retreat with Thomas Merton

A Seven-Day Spiritual Journey

Esther de Waal

With a New Foreword by Bonnie B. Thurston

LITURGICAL PRESS
Collegeville, Minnesota

www.litpress.org

Cover design by Savanah N. Landerholm

Photograph of Thomas Merton by John Howard Griffin. Used with permission of the Merton Legacy Trust and the Thomas Merton Center, Bellarmine University.

Photographs by Thomas Merton. Used with permission of the Merton Legacy Trust and the Thomas Merton Center, Bellarmine University.

Originally published in the UK under the title *A Retreat with Thomas Merton* by Inter Publishing Service (IPS) Ltd, Third edition published in the UK by the Canterbury Press, an imprint of Hymns Ancient & Modern Ltd of 13a Hellesdon Park Road, Norwich, Norfolk NR6 5DR.

Esther de Waal asserts the moral right to be identified as the Author of this Work.

1	2	3	4	5	6	7	8	9

Library of Congress Cataloging-in-Publication Data

Names: De Waal, Esther, 1930- author.
Title: A retreat with Thomas Merton : a seven-day spiritual journey / Esther de Waal.
Other titles: Seven day journey with Thomas Merton
Description: Collegeville, Minnesota : Liturgical Press, 2023. | Originally published in the UK under the title A Retreat with Thomas Merton by Inter Publishing Service (IPS) Ltd in 1992. First US edition published as A seven day journey with Thomas Merton by Servant Publications in 1993. | Includes bibliographical references. | Summary: "In this book, Esther de Waal devises a seven-day personal or group retreat program using excerpts from Thomas Merton's writings and a selection of the photography for which he was also renowned. She creates a retreat that can be made at home, at a retreat center, on vacation, or over a week or longer"— Provided by publisher.
Identifiers: LCCN 2023021178 (print) | LCCN 2023021179 (ebook) | ISBN 9798400800351 (trade paperback) | ISBN 9798400800368 (epub) | ISBN 9798400800375 (pdf)
Subjects: LCSH: Spiritual life—Catholic Church. | Spiritual retreats. | Merton, Thomas, 1915-1968. | Catholic Church—Doctrines. | BISAC: RELIGION / Spirituality | RELIGION / Christian Living / Spiritual Growth
Classification: LCC BX2350.2 D4833 2023 (print) | LCC BX2350.2 (ebook) | DDC 248.4/82—dc23/eng/20230605
LC record available at https://lccn.loc.gov/2023021178
LC ebook record available at https://lccn.loc.gov/2023021179

It is essential to experience all the times
and moods of one good place.

Contents

New Foreword

Sometimes the best approach is by indirection. I learned this watching a wren build her nest. She never flew directly to it but, like a sail boat tacking in the wind, zig-zagged to her destination. This both protected the wren and engaged the observer's interest. A similar technique characterizes Esther de Waal's approach in this book. At the outset in practical notes for the reader, she explains this "is not a book about Thomas Merton," and yet the biographical section "Thomas Merton's Journey" is one of the most concise and perceptive essays on his life. By the time one has prayed through the retreat's seven "talks," one has come to know Merton at a more profound level than the facts of his biography, and perhaps Esther de Waal as well.

This is a book about prayer, demonstrating, she suggests, "the succession of steps taken by one woman in trying to draw closer to God with Merton's help." Hers is not only scholarly knowledge, but the fruit of practical experience as a wife, the mother of four (remarkable) sons, and decades of dedication to the church and the spiritual deepening of Christians of every ilk and on many continents.

The author addresses the reader as she might a friend, in the comfortable, intimate, quietly serious tone that characterizes much of de Waal's spiritual writing. What she says of Merton, that "[h]e meets us in simplicity and friendship," applies to her own work. Trained as an academic historian, she has written especially perceptively on Christian monastic traditions and Celtic Christianity. Her writing is without jargon, cant, or facile cliché. She never "talks down" to her audience, but invites us in and becomes, herself, an entrée to a deeper, more embodied life of prayer and, in this book, understanding of Merton.

The book is best used as it was intended: as a seven-day retreat, or perhaps as seven reflections in any time of retreat. "Day One" begins with the call to set aside time in order to reacquaint us with ourselves, to face ourselves, and thus our sinfulness, honestly. The second reflection is "a time for honesty." The compunction which arises from such self awareness leads one to explore interior solitude, what Merton calls "the true self" and, in the third reflection, its fundamental dependence upon God.

"Day Four," the central day of the retreat, focuses on "Encounter with Christ" through the lens not only of Merton, but of Guerric of Igny and Isaac of Stella. De Waal believes authentic encounter with Christ "is a movement into the obscurity, the loneliness and the sorrow of the Christ on Calvary." This is logically followed in "Day Five" by an exploration of the demands of love. What one might term "Christology lived within" occurs in the context of the "Common and Natural and Ordinary," title of the sixth reflection, reminding us "we must start where we are" and with what Merton called "an unspeakable reverence for the holiness of created things."

The final meditation invites us to integration by reflecting on the fact that Merton's was, as ours is, a life-long search to bring, and hold together within, that which is life giving. We must avoid being distracted in favor of living from a "hidden wholeness" which, as Merton wrote in a letter to students at Smith College, is a "hidden ground of Love." (Merton's capital letter.)

Merton was a monastic and religious polymath. He knew a lot about a lot. As a result, his writing has been used for many purposes. Groups and movements have co-opted him to support their own agendas. De Waal's book allows Merton to be Merton. It keeps the reader's attention clearly on the essential Merton, the spiritual pilgrim, monk, and man of prayer. His work is quoted so skillfully that one hardly notices how extensive is de Waal's knowledge of his numerous publications. She not only "knows

Merton," but she "gets him," and introduces him with an attractive indirection. "This is how I experience it," she says in effect, but by skillfully drawing on Merton's own words, she illuminates for us his understanding. Her own voice is clear, but her spotlight is always on Merton.

As she asserted at the outset, this is a book about prayer, "prayer" being short hand for the genuine desire for and search for God. Esther de Waal gives the coordinates of Merton's own map for the journey, as well as a personal, but never inappropriately confessional, record of her use of his directions. I am grateful Liturgical Press is offering this new edition of her book and experience of Merton. It is both an engaging summary of Merton's spirituality and a moving and encouraging record of its effects in the life of a learned, articulate, and spiritually generous woman.

We can never be reminded often enough that our "Christology," our understanding of Jesus, and the spiritual convictions which flow from it, must be lived and manifested in our daily circumstances and ordinary lives. The methodologically gentle indirection of de Waal's retreat corrects one aspect of this conviction by demonstrating that no life, male or female, monastic, clerical, or laity, is "ordinary" because every person is potentially *theotokos*, a God-bearer. For this we were born, and for it we need the assistance of midwives like the two in this book.

Bonnie B. Thurston

Bonnie Thurston wrote one of the first Ph.D. dissertations on Merton, was a founding member and past president of the International Thomas Merton Society, and is author of many articles on Merton and *Shaped by the End You Live For: Thomas Merton's Monastic Spirituality.*

Foreword

What better guide than Thomas Merton on a seven day spiritual journey! Esther de Waal realised that Thomas Merton would be able to help her to hear God's call, to respond to it generously, to find her true self, to meet the living Christ, to understand the demands of love, to faithfully live the ordinary of every day and to gradually grow into spiritual wholeness.

While being a solitary person, Thomas Merton was so well connected with the society of his time, that he can truly touch the heart of contemporary men and women who search for God.

I am glad that this book not only contains Merton's words but also his pictures, since both words and pictures convey in such a powerful way what it means to be folly involved in the world without belonging to it. Merton himself was a very earthy as well as a very spiritual man.

My own encounter with Merton is a good illustration of this. In 1966 while spending a few days at the Abbey of Gethsemani, Joe Ahearn, a friend from the University of Notre Dame, who also was a guest, said: "I am going to see Thomas Merton this afternoon, would you like to join me?" Strangely enough I was not very eager to meet Merton. I had read *The Seven Storey Mountain* years ago in Holland, but no other of Merton's books and I wasn't sure if I had anything to say to him or ask him. But Joe insisted: "Come" he said, "you will enjoy meeting Tom. He told me to get a six-pack of beer and meet him at the pond."

A few hours later the three of us got together. Merton looked like a farmer interrupting his work in the barn. He was dressed in blue jeans and a workman's shirt and talked in a very down-to-earth way about people and events that came up in the conversation. Nothing pious, nothing "spiritual," nothing very "uplifting." It really seemed that Merton did everything to make us forget that he was one of the most known and respected spiritual writers of his time. There was a bit of a "naughty boy" about him, someone who was not too happy with the adults and looked for little ways to get around them.

I forgot most of what we talked about. Only vague memories of a discussion on Albert Camus and some speculations about the next Abbot of Gethsemani remain in my mind. What I will always retain however is the image of this big, open, utterly normal man, who enjoyed a can of beer with two of his guests.

Less than two years later Merton was dead. Only then my seemingly insignificant hour with him started to bear fruit. Our chance meeting made me read all his books, and I discovered that this ordinary man was a true guide to the heart of God and the heart of this world.

When I read Esther de Waal's *A Seven Day Journey with Thomas Merton*, I said to myself: "What better guide can there be than this earthy, yet so spiritual man, whom I met with my friend Joe at the pond in Gethsemani."

Henri J. M. Nouwen

Introduction

Thomas Merton defies time and place and any attempt at categorisation. Starting his monastic life in the season of Advent he continued to live on the cusp of light and darkness. The holding together of contradictory forces is an image characteristic of this amazing man; the solitary who loved company, the hermit who was an activist, the academic who was a poet and a photographer. The fact that a book which brings together his verbal skill and his artistic talent is now being reissued is a testimony to the fact that he continues to speak to the minds and hearts of great numbers of people today. By a strange serendipity I am writing this new introduction on December 10th, the date of my birthday. December 10th was the day on which, in 1941, Thomas Merton entered the abbey of Gethsemani, in Kentucky, to become a Trappist monk, and it was also the day in 1968 on which he died so tragically in Bangkok. This coincidence has always seemed to carry a special significance for me, one of many links I felt had brought me close to this most extraordinary man who has proved to be friend, guide and inspiration for so many throughout the world. I cannot now remember how I first discovered Merton but I have a vivid memory of choosing *Seeds of Contemplation* as my Lent reading when I was still a student. Here I found a man who could open doors, show me a glimpse of the way, stir my imagination and draw me into dimensions of faith which were new, yet totally unthreatening to my earlier Christian experience. I was brought up in an Evangelical country vicarage in an atmosphere which had offered few opportunities for me to explore the riches of the monastic tradition, whether of the past or present. Here was a man who spoke to me then and who has continued to accompany me on my Christian journey. His writings have playing an important part in my own life, and it seemed entirely natural that I should turn to him for help and guidance in undertaking this seven-day journey of prayer, silence and time with God.

The pattern of this retreat is entirely of my own devising. It has not been dictated by anything other than what I perceived as my own need to be refreshed and to gain some new perspectives in my life. It is of course essentially about finding time for prayer and that I believe involves that sight, imagination and senses. That is why the photographs play such an important part. Merton himself became an enthusiastic photographer and used his camera to express his love of God and of God's world. I believe that if we come to see how he saw the world we also learn much about the way in which he prayed. I am extremely grateful to the Merton Center of Bellarmine College, Louisville and to the Merton Legacy Trust for their helpful advice and for permission to reproduce here some of Merton's photographs.

December 10, 2010
Cwm Cottage
Rowlestone,
Pontrilas Herefordshire

How Do I Use This Time?

Some Practical Notes

For many of us the chance to take time off to spend a week or even a week-end away is an almost impossible luxury; we can afford neither the time nor the money. Yet if I am to take myself seriously, to respect the whole of myself, body, mind and spirit, and acknowledge how vital it is to nurture myself, I know that time apart is essential. It is essential to find time to stand back, to draw breath, not only for my own sake but also for my relationships with my family, colleagues, friends, and above all for an ever deepening relationship with God. If the purpose of having this time is merely to run away, to escape, then it will do me no good. Merton knows this and he warns me about it. "We have to remember that we look for solitude in order to grow there in love for God and in love for others. We do not go into the desert to escape people but to learn how to find them: we do not leave them in order to have nothing more to do with them, but to find out the way to do them the most good. But this is always only a secondary end. The one end that includes all others is the love of God." When Merton writes about the need for solitude in his own life he is also speaking on behalf of all of us as we become aware of that need in ourselves.

If this is going to be a real priority, then somehow or other I shall have to try to make time, whether by setting aside perhaps an hour or so every morning for a week or alternatively one whole morning a week over a couple of months. Whatever that is will obviously be dictated by my circumstances, as well as by the space which I can make available. Perhaps one corner of a room can become a small place of prayer, marked out with pictures or an icon. A lighted candle is always good. Perhaps there will be some objects such as stones or bits of wood, possibly suggested by the photographs, which I shall add as time goes on. If it is summer there may well be a place out of doors which lends itself as a suitable secluded spot. Maybe there is a side chapel in a nearby church where it is possible for me to spend time undisturbed. Wherever it is to be, the one essential is that it is a place in which it is possible to be quiet and on my own. "Learn to be alone" is the title of one of the chapters of *New Seeds of Contemplation*, and in it Merton has some practical and profoundly wise advice. Find the place he tells us, and once you have found it, be content with it, "love it, and return to it as soon as you can, and do not be too quick to change it for another." And then make a real effort to put aside all noise, both the outer and the inner.

> You should be able to untether yourself from the world
>   and set yourself free,
> loosing all the fine strings and tensions that bind you,
>   by sight,
>   by sound,
>   by thought,
>   to the presence of others.
> . . . Let there be a place somewhere in which you can
>   breathe naturally, quietly,
> and not to have to take your breath in continuous short
>   gasps.
> A place where your mind can be idle and forget its
> concerns,
> descend into silence,
> and worship the Father in secret.

It might be a good thing to open our eyes and see.

This is not as easy as it sounds. It is not easy to switch off. I find myself making lists of things I need to do, in the grip of distracting thoughts, and continuing inner conversations, particularly any in which I feel myself to be the injured party, misunderstood and undervalued. This is of course something only too familiar to monks and hermits as they also struggle to centre themselves on God in solitude. St Benedict knew very well the hazards of what he called "murmuring." Commenting on this Merton gave the original Latin word its old English translation, grouching, griping, like cramps in the stomach, a kind of cramp or spasm that gets into the soul. It really is a vice, and like any vice it can get a grip. Perhaps today we can see that it is a form of addiction, and like any addiction needs to be rooted out, and that is something for which we need help. First and foremost I seek God's help by throwing myself on His mercy and asking for His grace to uphold me in the coming time. But I also turn for practical help so that I can learn to become still both in body and mind. The way in which I sit or breathe are simple but fundamentally important aspects of how I pray and I am grateful that more and more we are being told about the importance of the posture of the body in prayer.

There are certain entirely practical things you can do. First of all decide in what position you can best pray. It need no longer be stiffly upright on your knees which I thought in my childhood was the only proper way to approach God. Now I know that there is no necessary connection between physical discomfort and holy thoughts. So sit, or kneel, or lie, or use a prayer stool. Its important to be entirely realistic. If you choose a position which after a short time gives you cramp or pins and needles all that you will be aware of is your jarring body.

Then, when you are completely relaxed (don't rush, there's all the time in the world) concentrate on your breathing. Take deep, slow breaths. Perhaps you might like to imagine breathing out all your frustrations, distractions, anxieties, and breathing in all the good gifts of God, gentleness, serenity. You may find it helpful to repeat a word, for example the name of Jesus, over and over again, to deepen your sense of rhythm. This is where a lighted candle will probably bring a point of focus. If your time is limited be entirely practical again in setting an alarm or timer to go off which will tell you when the time is up. This will allow you to relax more completely and to enter more fully into your interior silence. Whatever you do let it be something which is easy, which feels natural and which you enjoy so much that, at the end of each daily time, you look forward to the next.

At the same time we should be careful about getting caught up in too many techniques and methods. There are endless books, tapes, pamphlets, courses available today on the whole subject of prayer. In his usual straightforward way Merton tells us that if we want to pray, really want to pray, then the best thing is simply to get on with it. "Nothing that anyone says will be that important. The great thing is prayer. Prayer itself. If you want a life of prayer, the way to get to it is by praying." He was talking to a small group of men and women in California who had asked him about prayer. "We already know a great deal about it." "Now we need to grasp it."

This book is meant to become prayer. It is given to help to get you started and the use you make of it must be entirely your own for this is the only way it can work in you and for you. It is not a book about Thomas Merton. It simply shows the succession of steps taken by one woman in trying to draw closer to God with Merton's help. I do not follow any accepted scheme or pattern, but have devised something which seemed to make sense for my own needs at the time, turning to passages from Merton's writings as a guide, and finding that his photographs were also an important part of the whole. I also include a number of passages from those earlier monastic writers who were so important to Merton, "my fathers and friends" as he once called them, for they have given me much practical wisdom. And I have used the psalms. They have always been very important in my own life, just as they played such a central part in Merton's life at Gethsemani. There the monks meditated on them as they sang them daily in choir. "It was a question of 'savouring' and 'absorbing' the meaning of

the psalms in the depths of one's heart" he once said, "repeating
the words slowly, thoughtfully, prayerfully in the deepest center
of one's being, so that the psalms gradually come to be as intimate
and personal as one's own reflections and feelings."

In telling us this he is giving us excellent advice on how we too
can turn to the psalms in the next few days. Merton once told a
fellow monk that he liked "to get lost in the psalms and try to let
them be in my heart, so that before the Lord I am this psalm and
nothing else." His book about the psalms *Bread in the Wilderness*
has many good things to say:

> They are bread, miraculously provided by Christ, to
> feed those who have followed Him into the wilderness.

> The psalms acquire, for those who know how to enter
> into them, a surprising depth, a marvellous and inex-
> haustible actuality.

> The psalms bring our hearts and minds into the *pres-
> ence* of the living God.

> The psalms are at the same time the simplest and the
> greatest of all religious poems.

What he says about savouring and absorbing, repeating slowly
in the depths of the heart, thoughtfully and prayerfully, is wise
advice equally applicable to any of the material included here. It is
meant to be handled as the monks would handle their daily reading of the scriptures, read slowly, cradled and rocked in the heart as
one would cradle and rock a small child. (The idea of rhythm that
this suggests may be helpful for some people.) The really important
thing is that if any paragraph or phrase or just one single word,
strikes a note, stop at that point, linger there, staying with what
it has to say to you. Quoting one of the Fathers, Theophane the
Recluse, Merton tells us to beware of running from one thought to

the next but "give each one time to settle in the heart." It is better to stop reading at that point, turn that thought over and over in your mind, absorbing it, resting in it without effort and then when it seems natural and right passing quietly on. I like that idea of a gentle rocking movement in which the word or phrase is lovingly held like a small child. The gentleness is most important. To strive or to strain for results, or to feel that by now you should be getting somewhere, achieving something, is the wrong approach. It is important to be relaxed about what is happening. Time is not important. "Above all, don't be worried about the pace," Merton tells us, "about what is happening or not happening, about what seems to be going on on the surface. Hand that over to God, and believe that below the surface your mind and will and heart are being drawn into a place where God is at work—only pray that he will use the time in his own way. God is the source of your prayer."

> We live in the fullness of time.
> Every moment is God's own good time, his *kairos*
> The whole thing boils down to giving ourselves in
>   prayer a chance to realise that we have what we
>   seek.
> We don't have to rush after it.
> It is there all the time,
>   and if we give it time it will make itself known to us.

Your prayer may be helped if you keep a simple journal or notebook, and at the end of the allotted time record whatever has been most valuable and meaningful. Ideas and insights which are so vivid when you come to the end of a period of silent prayer can very easily get lost and overlaid later on. The journal should simply be honest notes which will be seen only by you. It will do no good to pretend to be anyone else or to have deeply moving spiritual thoughts which might more easily belong to a plaster saint. Simply make brief, laconic jottings as a memorandum to yourself. Some people may prefer to express what has happened visually. Even those who do not think that they can draw can pick up paints or crayons, take a large piece of paper, and show in colour and line what they feel. This can be particularly rewarding if it is done each day so that when your seven-day journey is at its end the pattern of what has been happening is there in front of you.

Perhaps slow, careful, meditative walking, feeling yourself particularly aware of sight and sound and touch, might play a natural part during the time. This can be wherever you are, there is no need to feel that you have to go and find some romantic scene: pavements and brick walls and city skylines can do perfectly well. Some people may already find this to be an easy and attractive way of praying; others might like to try and discover it if they have not tried it before. The following notes may be of help to anyone who might like to try an awareness walk.

First of all walk slowly, deliberately. You are going to use all your five senses as you walk, so start by being aware of the light, the warmth of the sun, the touch of the air, the colours around you.

Then begin to notice greater detail in patterns, shapes, thickness, the shades of colours, the contrasts and juxtapositions and how things relate.

Touch and feel, pick up stones, twigs, earth, leaves and hold them gently. If it's sensible take off your shoes and walk barefoot.

Try to stop thinking and simply to be. Let everything drop away and instead try to be totally present to what is reaching you through your senses.

Begin to notice smell more acutely, the scent of growing things, of the earth itself. Listen to the range of sounds, far off distant sounds, those which are close, your own breathing.

You may want at the end of the walk to bring back something that you have particularly enjoyed and place it in your place of prayer.

Perhaps you will feel that you must end with a thanksgiving exercise in which you quite consciously list the things you have discovered that God has given to you during the walk.

Merton's photographs are included as an integral part of this retreat. Of course how you use them will vary. The important thing is to spend time with them. He has this gift of taking the most ordinary and natural and commonplace things and seeing them so gently, with love and respect, that I think he can help us all to do the same. But, like everything else in this book, there is no particular way which is intrinsically better than any other. Simply ask God to show you which is His way for you at this time.

Before I go any further into this retreat I ask God's grace to find the time, the silence, the gentleness and sensitivity to be open to receive that which will be given to me in word and in sight. My prayer is that I may approach this time with open heart, with open mind, with open eyes and that through it I may become more deeply aware of God's presence in my life.

Words and Pictures

It might be a good thing to open our eyes and see.

It is essential to experience all the times
and moods of one good place.
It is God's love that warms me in the sun
and God's love that sends the cold rain.
It is God's love that feeds me in the bread I eat
and God's love that feeds me also by hunger
and fasting . . . It is God who breathes on me
with light winds off the river
and in the breezes out of the wood.

As we go about the world everything we meet
and everything we see and hear and touch . . .
plants in us . . . something of heaven.

It is good and praiseworthy to look at some real
created thing and feel and appreciate its reality.
Just let the reality of what is real sink into you . . .
for through real things we can reach Him
who is infinitely real.

A tree gives glory to God by being a tree.
For in being what God means it to be
it is obeying Him . . . The more a tree is like itself
it is like Him. This particular tree will give glory
to God by spreading out its roots in the earth
and raising its branches into the air
and the light in a way that no other tree
before or after it ever did or will do.

There is in all things an inexhaustible sweetness
and purity, a silence that is a fount of action
and joy. It rises up in wordless gentleness and flows
out to me from the unseen roots of all created being,
welcoming me tenderly, saluting me
with indescribable humility.

If I am supposed to hoe a garden or make a table,
then I will be obeying God if I am true to the task
that I am performing. To do the work carefully
and well, with love and respect for the nature
of my task and with due attention to its purpose,
is to unite myself to God's will in my work.
In this way I become His instrument.
He works through me.

The sun on the grass was beautiful.
Even the ground seemed alive.

Thomas Merton's Journey

Thomas Merton was born in January 1915 in Prades at the foot of the French Pyrenees, in a room whose window looked directly up to those mountains, where two great monasteries Saint Martin-du-Canigou and Saint Michel-de-Cuxa had stood since the Middle Ages. Later in life his mind would often go back with great reverence to "the thought of those clean, ancient cloisters, those low and mighty rounded arches hewn and set in place by monks who have perhaps prayed me where I am now." Both his parents were artists. Owen, his New Zealand father, was sufficiently successful to make the family living by the sale of his paintings. Merton's early years were divided between Europe and America where his mother's parents lived. In 1921, when he was only six, his mother died of cancer, a particularly traumatic experience since, apparently unable to bear him visiting her in this condition, she only wrote a note to him to say goodbye, and never let him see her before her death. Left now with two young sons, the younger boy John Paul was three at this time, Owen travelled widely. In 1925 John Paul was left behind with the American grandparents while Thomas and his father went to live in the south of France, in the medieval city of St Antonin. Thomas was now ten and these years made a very deep impression on him. One of his earliest memories was of how a labyrinth of narrow streets, lined by thirteenth-century houses, converged on the church so that its steeple dominated the town: "Here, in this amazing, ancient town, the very pattern of the place, of the houses and streets and of nature itself, the circling hills, the cliffs and trees, all focused my attention upon the one, important, central fact of the church and what it contained. Here, everywhere I went, I was forced, by the disposition of everything around me, to be always at least virtually conscious of the church. Everything here seemed to announce: 'This is the meaning of all created things: we have been made for no other purpose than that men may use us in raising themselves to God, and in proclaiming the glory of God.'"

Yet he still had no sense of what this might mean in his own life for his father was not a conventional believer and traditional religion played no part at all in Thomas' upbringing. In 1928 he was sent to live with an aunt in England to go first to a prep school in Surrey, and then when he was fourteen to Oakham. Here, in a minor English public school, whose ethos seemed to be principally concerned with producing "gentlemen," there was nothing to nourish the religious sensibilities of a sensitive and artistic boy. And now his father was also now dying, and with his death "that hard crust of my soul finally squeezed out all the last traces of religion that had ever been in it." But in the summer of 1933, taking a holiday in Europe before going up to Clare College, Cambridge, he went to Rome, and there as he explored the city he saw the Byzantinelike mosaics of Christ in their magnificent settings and found himself being drawn into churches not simply for the art but for the sense of peace he experienced there. "For the first time in my life I began to find out something of who this Person was that men call Christ." And here for the first time in his life he began to pray, "praying out of the very roots of my life and of my being, and praying to the God I had never known . . . ."

All this however was to be lost in the year that followed at Cambridge. He plunged into a life of parties, drinking, girlfriends, which he was later to describe as "a huge bite of this rotten fruit." It was hardly surprising that at the end of the year his guardian should send him back to finish his university studies in New York.

At Columbia however the pattern repeated itself and he threw himself into jazz, parties, politics, more drinking, more talking, more girlfriends. But he also wrote, and discovered William Blake and made many friends who were later to play an important part in his life. And, by buying a book on medieval philosophy that he saw by chance in a shop window, he stumbled into becoming a Christian. His journey into God was now beginning. "I desire only one thing: to love God. Those who love him keep his commandments. I only desire to do one thing: to follow his will. I pray that I am at least beginning to know what that may mean. Could it possibly mean that I might some day become a monk?" He first thought of joining the Franciscans but when that came to nothing he faced the idea that he might become a Trappist, the strict Cistercians, whose life was marked by austerity and silence.

On December 10, 1941, when he was twenty-six, Thomas Merton came to the gates of the abbey of Gethsemani in Kentucky and asked to enter. He was never to leave. He had come home. Not that it was by any means easy. His whole life was to continue to be a struggle. It was here however that he knew he belonged. He had a gift for prayer and this was a place in which prayer was the most important thing. The monastic timetable was marked by the shared prayer recited in common in church seven times a day, which began with getting up while it was still dark in the middle of the night, and after that gathering at intervals to praise God throughout the rest of the day until it was time for Compline, the final service at about 7 p.m. before retiring to bed. It was because of this that the psalms became so important to him. During a week the monks would chant the entire psalter. They came to live them and experience them as their own prayers, their own songs. They found, as they said them day and night, year in and year out, that they entered into every department of their lives, became continual nourishment in daily life. We shall come back to the role of the psalms, for just as they played such a large role in Merton's life so too they are to play an important part in our own time of prayer and silence.

At Gethsemani his abbot asked Merton to continue with his writing, even though a writing career was a little unusual for a monk. But as Father Louis, (he had changed his name on entering the community), a monk under the vow of obedience, he had no choice, even though he had intended to give all that up. He was told to write his autobiography, and this he did, the story of a twentieth-century man who followed all the avenues that promised a full and fulfilling life, and eventually found that the road led him to this place of poverty, prayer and silence. *The Seven Storey Mountain*, published in the UK as *Elected Silence*, was an immediate success and became a best seller almost overnight. Thousands found that they could identify with Merton and with his journey. Through it many discovered the Christian faith and a large number explored a monastic vocation. "I felt that this story was my story" a young Englishman told one of Merton's friends, "I followed Thomas Merton's path and I reached the end of it, just as he did."

From then on Merton never stopped writing. Books, articles, poems, flowed from his pen. He wrote books of meditation, books about the monastic life, books on issues of peace and war, books on Zen and the East. Yet he managed to avoid the danger which besets all well-known authors, of writing to fulfil their readers' expectations. In each successive book he seems to manage to destroy something of the image of himself that he had established in his earlier writing. Here we watch a man living openly and freely, always moving on, exploring new areas, never limited by stereotypes, or bound by other people's expectations.

Merton wrote because he had to write. For him his writing and his life of prayer were inseparable. He needed both in order to live. Prayer was essential for this was the way in which he could know God most fully. He was a writer because this was the way in which he could express himself most fully. He says of his writing in *The Sign of Jonas*, the journal of his early years at Gethsemani, "To put myself down on paper—in complete simplicity and integrity—without exaggeration, repetition, useless emphasis—It is a kind of crucifixion—It must come somehow from the Holy Ghost."

Part of that crucifixion was "losing myself entirely by becoming public property." Yet in the last resort none of us really know the secret Merton, the man whose life was hidden in Christ. He does however allow us to intrude a very long way. He is generous in giving himself to us, just as in his own life he was generous in making himself so constantly available to all the visitors who came from the ends of the earth to see him and in replying to those endless correspondents from every walk of life who wrote to him.

Right from the start he found within himself a deep and intense need for more and more time for prayer in solitude. Time and again his letters and journals reveal this as the most profound thirst, welling up from his depths. In *The Sign of Jonas* he says, "I have only one desire and that is the desire for solitude—to disappear into God. . . . It is clear to me that solitude is my vocation, not as flight from the world, but as my place in the world." In the end his request was granted and a small cinder block hermitage was made available in the woods not far from the monastery. It was here in August 1965, twenty four years after he first entered the community, that the abbot, James Fox, gave him permission to live as a full-time hermit. While this is part of the traditional monastic life, the very word monk coming from *monos*, meaning solitary, at this time most monks and nuns were living together in community. By choosing the eremitical life he was making an important statement about the need for solitude, a need which has since then been increasingly widely recognised and acknowledged. In writing about his life in the hermitage Merton was also helping anyone to follow in his or her Christian life today. Time apart, time in solitude, time to be alone with God is vital for us all. We should not dismiss it as irrelevant for those of us living our ordinary, busy lives in the world, something remote and impossible except for those choosing to live as hermits. "Solitude is not found so much by looking outside the boundaries of your dwelling, as by staying within. Solitude is not something you must hope for in the future. Rather, it is a deepening of the present, and unless you look for it in the present you will never find it." This is why Merton becomes such a valuable guide for anyone who wants to find time in order to draw closer to God.

Here in this simple hermitage in the woods near the monastery Merton spent the last three years of his life. "There is nothing left for me but to live fully and completely in the present, praying when I pray, and writing and praying when I write, and worrying about nothing but the will and the glory of God, finding these as best I can in the sacrament of the present moment." It was therefore an extraordinary thing when he was given permission to address a meeting of monks and theologians in Bangkok. His interest had increasingly turned to Eastern monastic tradition, and he was immensely grateful at the prospect of being able to travel and to see something of this for himself. It was because he had by now found a home that he was ready to go out. He knew that he belonged at Gethsemani, and that this rootedness gave him a place from which to set out and to which to return.

All his life Merton was open to the new: "open," "wide open" are amongst his favourite words. So all the new sights and people were enormously exciting. The journey there was already in itself sufficiently exhilarating—New Mexico and the Redwoods, California, then finally Asia where the highlight was a memorable visit to the great Buddhist statues at Polonnaruwa in Sri Lanka. On the morning of December 10, 1968 (it was twenty-seven years to the day since he had entered Gethsemani), he addressed his fellow participants at the conference, speaking to them among other things of the monastic vow of conversion of life, *conversatio morum*, under which he lived. He described it as the most essential but also the most mysterious of the vows. He said that for him it meant a commitment to total inner transformation of one sort or another—a commitment to become a completely new person, a continuing pattern of dying and rebirth, of death and new life. Those words can now be seen as prophetic. For he went back to his room, took a shower and in doing so accidentally electrocuted himself.

As he was leaving the hall after his address somebody stopped him and told him that a nun in the audience was complaining that he had said nothing about converting people. His reply gives us his last words: "What we are asked to do at present is not so much to speak of Christ as to let Him live in us so that people may find Him by feeling how He lives in us." Here in effect he is giving us an overview of his life and his writing. A journey into Christ is a very clear way in which to see his life. As we read him we find that this journey is not simply his own personal journey, it is also a journey that we all recognise as our own, that inner journey we all must make. "Our real journey in life is interior: it is a matter of growth, deepening, and of an ever greater surrender to the creative action of love and grace in our hearts."

Life in the monastery, even in the hermitage, never separated Merton from pain and suffering, whether his own or that of the wider world. He never escaped what each of us has to face separately and corporately. "This journey without maps leads us into rugged mountainous country where there are often mists and storms and where we are more and more alone. Yet at the same time, ascending the slopes in darkness, finding more and more keenly our own emptiness, and with the winter wind blowing through our now tattered garments, we meet at times other travellers on the way, poor pilgrims as we are, and solitary as we. . . . We all find, however different we may be, that he speaks on our behalf, that we can identify with him." "Each of us knows a different Thomas Merton," said Naomi Burton, one of his closest friends who worked with him through his writing and publishing. He had this great gift of going out to each of his friends in a unique way—he touched each at his or her own level, answering their need, giving them his love. And for those of us who have come to know him through his writings it is the same. At whatever point we may be on our own particular journey we find that he seems to know what that journey entails.

In the preface to the Japanese edition of *Thoughts in Solitude*, which appeared towards the end of his life in 1966 when he writes of the fruitfulness of the solitary life he is undoubtedly telling us a great deal about himself. "He lives as a seed planted in the ground.

As Christ said, the seed in the ground must die. To be a seed in the ground of one's life is to dissolve in the ground in order to become fruitful. One disappears into Love, in order to 'be Love.' But this fruitfulness is beyond any planning and any understanding. To be 'fruitful' in this sense, one must forget every idea of fruitfulness or productivity and merely *be*." He then goes on to say that this is both an act of faith and an act of doubt. This appeals to me since that is how I too live and struggle with my own Christian life. I find in Merton a man who does not offer me certainties, who does not claim to have all the answers. "In fact I often wonder quite openly about the 'answers,' and about the habit of having them ready. The best I can do is to look for some of the questions." He meets us in simplicity and friendship. "I would not try to sell anybody anything. My function would be (as it must be in any case) to be a man of God, a man belonging to Christ, in simplicity, to be the friend of all those who are interested in spiritual things, whether of art or prayer, or anything *valid*, simply to be their friend, to be someone who could speak to them and to whom they could speak, to encourage one another."

In his own community he remained Father Louis, a monk among monks. He did not ask for or want any special attention. He was always very much himself, very alive and very real. After his death one of his fellow-monks spoke about living with him in community. "He was nothing if not real. And part of that reality was his simplicity, his being himself. He said what he thought and did what he thought should be done, and that was all there was to it. And what he said and what he did was rooted in love for God and man." In Bangkok Merton had said very vigorously, "I am a monk. I shall remain a monk until death. Nothing can stop me from being one." Rumours were circulating that he was about to leave, and indeed he would have been the first to recognise how unlikely a monk he was. And yet that too was part of it—his vocation was a gratuitous gift from God, and his perseverance in that calling, in spite of all the ups and downs and turmoil, was a continual, personal experience of God's gracious love. After his

solemn profession he had said, "I am part of Gethsemani. I belong
to the family. It is a family about which I have no illusions." Later
on he was to write about these early years in *The Sign of Jonas*
when he tried to present the Cistercian life not in ideal terms but
in the concrete reality of an actual monastery, with all its faults.
"We have never deceived ourselves by pretending to be angels on
earth, but we know that Christian perfection and union with God
must be realised in the treadmill of this daily life . . . that God,
in short, allows himself to be found *in normal life* provided this
life is truly the life of grace and that we endeavour to live it thoroughly, and with no pretence, seeking God and nothing else!" It
is just because monastic life is so concrete and normal, because it
is founded on hard-won experience rather than on abstract principles or concepts, that it can speak to all of us, whoever we may
be and wherever we may be. Monastic life does not mean escape
from all the ordinary difficulties that face ordinary people living
a normal humdrum life in the world. In the monastery one has to
face the inescapable realities of learning to live with oneself and to
live with other people, and of trying to make the daily routine of
all those inescapable responsibilities, cooking, chores, administra-
tion, proper upkeep of property and possessions, become a way of
finding God in and through the daily and the material.

Merton's own writing comes out of his exploration of the whole
monastic tradition which he continually mined for further insight
into his own spiritual life. "It seems to me that we all need more
and more to deepen the grasp we have of our rich monastic heritage, and the closer we get to the source, the more fruitful and
splendid our lives will be" he wrote to a friend who was a Benedictine monk. In one of the introductions to his books he told
readers not to expect here anything that smacked of newness, but
rather "a return to the ancient sources, a renewal in the sense of a
recovery of that which has permanent significance, of that which
is eternally true." So he returned to the Rule of St Benedict, to St
Bernard and the early Cistercians, to the early Desert Fathers, and
towards the end of his life to the monastic understanding of the

East, but "above all a return to the Gospel of Jesus Christ." For as he said in his preface to an edition of the Christmas sermons of the twelfth-century Cistercian Guerric of Igny, "Here is the Gospel message in all its original simplicity, undyingly new: the message that men and women are really loved by God, that sins are really forgiven, and that the mercy of God, beyond all our comprehension, has come to drive out forever the bitterness of selfish hearts and fill us instead with the sweetness of His presence forever."

The message of love, the primacy of love, this is the most basic definition of monastic life as Merton discovered it, lived it and shows it to us. In the sixth century St Benedict had written a rule to show monks and nuns how to live together in love for one another and for God, a simple rule which guided thousands of men and women throughout the Middle Ages, as it does today. The reforms of St Bernard in the twelfth century were intended to recall men to the purity of that rule and its understanding of love. The very name that was given to the document that established the Cistercian order, Charter of Charity, is a statement of that priority. But if the purpose of the Cistercian life as Merton lived it is of wholehearted openness to love lived out daily in his community surely that is no different from what I, or any of us, live out in marriage, family, office, parish or whatever may be the circumstances in which we find ourselves. And if Merton found that this was a life-long task with which he had to struggle, there again I feel that I can identify with him.

When he entered the monastery Merton made the promise of stability, to stay there for the rest of his life. It was paradoxically this safe base that allowed him to make both the inner and the outer journey. Not only was he at home "in one good place" as he once put it, but also, more profoundly, he was at home in himself. He was no longer trying to run away from himself along all those escape routes that he had followed one after another in his earlier years. The promise of conversion of life or *conversatio morum* meant a commitment to follow Christ along the road of discipleship, wherever that might lead or whatever it might cost—that quest for continual transformation until death that he spoke of on the last day of his life. These two very simple and basic concepts, of staying still in my innermost centre and not trying to escape, and yet at the same time reaching out from there to journey on, to grow into the person God wants me to be, are concepts to which I shall return during this time of retreat. It will be time set apart each day in which to strengthen that inner centre, my deepest stability in the sense of not running away, either from myself or from God. During it I hope at the same time to move on, so that it is from stillness that moving forward, exploration, a journey becomes possible. And all this will ask of me that I listen to God, that I am open to His Word in whatever way it may reach me—something which was also fundamental in Merton's monastic life, and to which he was committed by his promise of obedience, since obedience ultimately means hearing the Word and saying Yes.

As I think about the three points around which Merton's monastic life moved they recall to me the three moments in the story of the prodigal son. He listens, hears and responds to the voice of God; he then sets out on the journey of conversion, turning and so returning to God; and then he comes home, home to his father, the place where he really belongs. This is my own story too, all our stories. We are each of us the prodigal, needing to hear God, needing to return to Him, to come home to those welcoming and forgiving hands held out to us, to the place where we most truly belong. This is the universal human experience.

∼

Merton respected matter, handled it gently, and did not try to impose or to possess. This probably stemmed from his gentle artist father and his early childhood in France. On the opening page of the autobiography he tells us of this debt. He writes of how his father *saw*. "His vision of the world was sane, full of balance, full of veneration for structure, for the relationships of masses and for all the circumstances that impress an individual identity on each created thing." Already, even though he did not yet recognise it, Merton was experiencing a sacramental view of the world, a world that told him about God even if at this date it was a God whose name he did not even know. For he was seeing the world through the eyes of a man whose "vision was religious and clean, and therefore his paintings were without decoration or superfluous comment, since a religious man respects the power of God's creation to bear witness for itself." Later in life he looked back and reflected on what this time in St Antonin had meant. "What a thing it is, to live in a place that is so constructed that you are forced, in spite of yourself, to be at least a virtual contemplative!"

In the 1950s his old friend John Howard Griffin, a professional photographer, had visited Merton in his hermitage and showed him his camera. Merton showed such childlike excitement that Griffin let him have the camera "on long loan." From then on photography became an absorbing interest. To photograph things became for him a form of meditation. In the introduction to *A Hidden Wholeness*, a collection of Merton's photographs, Griffin was to say of him, "He did not seek to capture or possess, and certainly not to arrange the objects he photographed. He lent his vision and his lenses to them in a real way; he was there and he did the mechanical things—focusing, composing—but he allowed the objects to remain true to themselves, and he trusted that the connections would somehow be made." For Merton the most important thing in life was to be all the time in the presence of God through prayer. Taking photographs was part of that. His photographs tell us much about the way in which he saw the world, how he handled the things of the world. If we take time with them they can give us something of his vision.

This is why Merton's photographs play such an important part in this book. They help me to be aware of the presence of God in things which otherwise I might pass by without noticing. Many of us might go in search of a rose, a sunset, and fail to notice a brick wall, the dead roots of a tree. Merton photographed the texture of the wood in the roots, the relationship of one simple thing to another, the shape and form of everything that came to hand in his immediate world. He did this, just as his father had painted, "without decoration or superfluous comment." Like his father he respected the power of God's creation to bear witness for itself. He went out to each thing, allowed it to communicate its essence, to say what it would, reveal what it would. He was always insistent on our need to "see directly what is in front of us." There is the sense here that we find in poets and artists that "the observed particulars take on the mystery of revelation." This asks of me to take time, to be sensitive to the thing itself, allowing it to be what it is and to say what it wants to say. Griffin tells us that for Merton the best images were silent. He used photography, as he used words, to explore silence. "The best images were silent but communicative. . . . He struggled toward an expression of silence through the visual image. . . . Merton held that it was not so much what you did that counted, but what you allowed to be done to yourself." He worked for photographic images which, when viewed without haste or pressure, might accomplish the slow work of communicating "a hidden wholeness," and perhaps reveal some hint of that wordless gentleness that flows out from "the unseen roots of all created being."

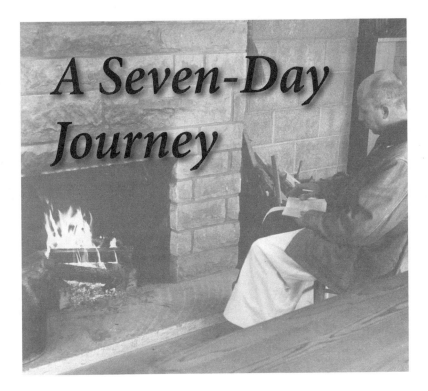

A Seven-Day
Journey

DAY ONE

The Call

This is a time apart, a time to be alone with myself and with God. I have given it to myself as gift but also as necessity, because I recognise that this is something that I need for myself, that I want to make a priority in my life at this moment. This is a time to acknowledge my total and utter dependence on God, my need for Him, my great longing for Him. This is a time to affirm myself before God, to find nurturing and recreation, so that, with His grace, I may deepen my inner resources. I am coming apart in order that I may find again, and strengthen, that person whom I most deeply and truly am before God. What I am setting out to do is risky—an encounter with myself and with God. I may meet my real self. I may meet the true God. Perhaps I have been running away from both. So now I commend this undertaking to God and pray that with His grace, and with the support and insight that I shall gain from the words of Thomas Merton, fellow-pilgrim on the journey, this may be a time for the deepening of love, faith and prayer.

> O Lord God,
> I have no idea where I am going,
> I do not see the road ahead of me,
> I cannot know for certain where it will end.

Nor do I really know myself, and that fact that I think
I am following Your will
does not mean that I am actually doing so.
But I believe
that the desire to please You
does in fact please You.
And I hope I have that desire
in all that I am doing.

I hope that I will never do anything
apart from that desire to please You.
And I know that if I do this
You will lead me by the right road,
though I may know nothing about it.
Therefore I will trust You always
though I may seem to be lost
and in the shadow of death.
I will not fear,
for You are ever with me,
and You will never leave me
to make my journey alone.

Who am I before God at this point in my life? At the start of this
time I present myself before God with empty hands. I recognise
my own nothingness and my complete dependence on Him; even
the urge to make this retreat comes from Him. And yet at the same
time I acknowledge the fullness and the riches that I am bringing,
so that simultaneously I rejoice in my own humanity. I stop and
I look at myself. These hands of mine that I hold out before Him,
so worn and used, are hands made by God to do His work in the
world. The whole of myself made to be part of His world, . . . I
am overawed to think of the person that I am, that unique person,
so lovingly created by God in all the fullness and riches of my own
individuality, a person made to be His daughter, His son.

O Lord you search me, and you know me,
you know my resting and my rising,
you discern my purpose from afar.
You mark when I walk or lie down,
all my ways lie open to you.

Before ever a word is on my tongue
you know it, O Lord, through and through.
Behind and before you besiege me,
your hand ever laid upon me.

For it was you who created my being
and knit me together in my mother's womb.
I thank you for the wonder of my being,
for the wonders of all your creation.
(Psalm 138 [139], verses 1-5, 13, 14)

∾

I am embarking on this journey because I have heard a call. I am called by name, by my own name, to live out my calling to be myself—not for my own sake but for the sake of God who is my Creator. I pray that I may hear God, the Word, in the depths of my being. This asks of me total stillness in His presence that I may listen, and that I may hear that call.

Contemplation is also the response to a call:
a call from Him Who has no voice,
and yet Who speaks in everything that is,
and Who, most of all, speaks in the depths of our own
being: for we ourselves are words of His.

But we are words that are meant to respond to Him,
to answer Him,
to echo Him,
and even in some way to contain Him and signify Him.

Contemplation is this echo.
It is a deep resonance in the inmost centre of our spirit
in which our very life loses its separate voice
and resounds with the majesty and the mercy
of the Hidden and Living One.

As Merton describes contemplation he shows it to me as a part
of life, realistic, accessible. He tells me that it is the natural life in
me that has been completed, elevated, transformed and fulfilled
in Christ by the Holy Spirit.

Contemplation is the awareness and realisation, even
in some sense the *experience* of what each Christian
obscurely believes. "It is now no longer I that live but
Christ lives in me."

The one thing that this asks of me is time. So I try not to strive
and not to lay any huge burdens or expectations upon myself.
Merton was always so insistent that everything is given already,
and that all that we need is simply to experience what we already
have. Now I realise that the start must be simply to stay still, to
accept myself where I find myself, to be open to the present. I put
aside all demanding techniques and technology, and I listen to
what Merton tells me with such loving gentleness.

In technology you have this horizontal progress where
you must start at one point and move to another and
then another. But that is not the way to build a life of

prayer. In prayer we discover what we already have. You start where you are and you deepen what you already have, and you realize that you are already there. We already have everything but we don't know it and we don't experience it. Everything has been given to us in Christ. All we need is to experience what we already possess.

So I recognise that the starting point is that I am HERE. That here is where I will get the answers. This sets the boundaries of what I am doing. I am being asked to go deeper into myself. It is time to stop running, in all the different directions which have seemed so attractive, and instead take time just to be. Merton goes on to say:

> If we really want prayer, we'll have to give it time. We must slow down to a human tempo and we'll begin to have time to listen. And as soon as we listen to what's going on, things will begin to take shape by themselves. But for this we have to experience time in a new way. . . . The reason why we don't take time is a feeling that we have to keep moving. This is a real sickness. Today time is a commodity, and for each one of us time is mortgaged . . . . We must approach the whole idea of time in a new way. We live in the fullness of time. Every moment is God's own good time, His *kairos*. The whole thing boils down to giving ourselves in prayer a chance to realise that we have what we seek. We don't have to rush after it. It is there all the time, and if we give it time it will make itself known to us.

What is already given to me is God's love and acceptance of me. Although I rest in the knowledge of this, indeed I know it as the very root of my being, I easily and often forget it. I slip back. My relationship with God needs constant renewal. I have become deaf to His voice, or give it only passing semi-attention. My love has become lukewarm. I fail to see the signs of His presence in everything around me. I now make this prayer for myself:

> that what is lukewarm will spring again into living
> flame,
> what is dry will become living water.
> What is deaf and blind will return to light and to life.

> It is true that our love for God
> easily falls into tepidity and aridity
> when we do not come unceasingly back
> to the knowledge of His love for us.
> In truth, it is His love
> which is at the same time the cause and the term of our
> loving knowledge of Him.
> It is His love that invites us to find Him everywhere,
> in the Scripture,
> in nature,
> in our own hearts,
> in our own duties
> in solitude!

If there is one persistent theme in Merton's life, and in his writing, it is his quest for solitude. "What I needed was the solitude to expand in breadth and depth and to be simplified out under the gaze of God more or less the way a plant spreads out its leaves in the sun" he told his friend Dan Walsh, explaining his wish to enter the religious life. He recognised this desire for solitude as a thirst in himself, and in doing so he points to the same need in all of us.

Few of us can embrace the solitude of a contemplative monk, but the need for some solitude is essential for all of us, not a luxury. Merton would say that we need solitude not for perfection but for simple survival in the life that God has given us. It is a return to the centre. It is not something remote, something to be thought of later on, in the future, when I am not so busy, under so much pressure. It is now.

> Solitude is not found so much by looking outside the
> boundaries of your dwelling, as by staying within.
> Solitude is not something you must hope for in the
> future.
> Rather, it is a deepening of the present, and unless you
> look for it in the present you will never find it.

"Without some sort of solitude there is and can be no maturity." For it is only as we confront ourselves in solitude, when we can be at ease in solitude with ourselves, that we have truly begun to live. This, as Merton was so insistent, is not escapist or self-indulgent. To spend time alone, time to find the ground of my being is going to help me to become a whole person and to make relationships of wholeness with those around me. "We have thinking to do and work to do which demands a certain silence and aloneness. We need time to do our job of meditation and creation." This is related to the natural cycle of the need for rest and for leisure which are fundamental to well-being. I need time to break away, to recollect and to reflect, to refresh powers, simply to reunite myself with my own centre.

> Solitude is not withdrawal from ordinary life. It is not
> apart from, above, better than ordinary life. On the
> contrary, solitude is the very ground of that life; simple,
> unpretentious, fully human activity by which we quietly

earn our daily living and share our experiences with a
few intimate friends. But we must learn to know and
accept the ground of our being. To most people, though
it is always there, it is unthinkable and unknown. Con-
sequently their life has no centre and no foundation.

As my own solitude moves into silence I pray that these days
will not lead me simply into external silence, but into that deeper,
interior silence, that silent emptiness where as Merton once said
"an immense depth of pure silence expands within." This could
be extremely alarming, for it might bring me face to face with all
those naked realities which only the empty spaces of the desert
reveal. Yet this is also the place where with Merton and many other
earlier hermits we wait for the fulfilment of God's promise. The
Desert Fathers came into the desert to discover the inner meaning
of their own existence which had lost its purpose and significance
in the busy life of the towns. There, in the desert, they sought the
answers which are not easy to come by, for they must be sought
in quiet, in repentance, in suffering. "For no-one can demand an
answer as by right, and each one must be prepared to accept an
answer that may be in many ways disconcerting. The suffering and
solitude of the desert life are, in the eyes of the Egyptian monks,
the price that has to be paid for such an ultimate solution to the
question of existence. The price is not too high." That was why
Merton loved the Desert Fathers so much. When he sent a copy
of his book *Wisdom of the Desert* to a close friend he called them
"these silent old men—you have already met them—one does not
grow tired of their conversations."

"If these men say little about God it is because they know that
when one has been close to His dwelling silence makes more sense
that a lot of words." That is why he turned to them himself and
drew from their experience and why he points me too in their
direction. "These monks insisted on remaining human and 'ordinary'. . . . The simple men who lived their lives out to a good

old age among the rocks and sands only did so because they had come into the desert to be themselves, their *ordinary* selves, and to forget a world that divided them from themselves. There can be no other valid reason for seeking solitude . . ."

~

After his death his friend, John Howard Griffin, went to live in Merton's hermitage to work on his papers in preparation for writing his biography. He kept a journal of that time there, a time of temporary silence and solitude, because he would return at intervals to his wife and family. It was as though Griffin became, at least for a short time, a lay hermit, something with which I can identify. He writes out of his experience of the demands that such an undertaking will make on anyone who enters into it with real honesty and commitment.

No need to hide it (the unconscious) here: here one is called to face squarely the realities of oneself: of one's body, or one's mind, one's conscious and unconscious life; not deliberately—it is just part of the solitary life, part of the natural transparency of self that is accomplished in silence and solitude when one does not try to direct or guide it, but simply goes along with it. . . . part of the filtering process that takes place within— removing the impediments to love, the inner murkiness.

As man has to be converted over again each hour, so man has to be aware of his profound vulnerability each moment, because the world demands in each an illusion of strength that amounts to an illusion of invulnerability: thus the illusion of growth that is not authentic growth. Here, where man gives himself over to the times of nature, to the inner silences as well as the surrounding ones—where a man just gives himself over—the growth is more natural, not that unspeakable hot-house growth of the world. The reality he faces is the reality of his vulnerability, which is why he can hardly escape the awareness of God's mercy; here, in the solitude and silence, the world's images, the "mystique" of what a hermit should be simply falls away . . .

If I read this prayerfully it helps me to admit my own vulnerability.

I think about my own need for a total honesty and for the strength to lay down illusions.

Above all I am forced to recognise my total dependency on God's mercy and grace.

So now I really am ready to hear Merton when he says

Keep still, and let Him do some work.

Perhaps in the end it simply amounts to becoming aware, to being totally present to this moment, to being ready to listen. It is all given. It is all waiting. It is available to us all the time as Merton was never tired of reminding us. As a monk he would always remember that "He who is of God hears the words of God" (John 8:47) for at the start of every day of his life he would sing those verses of the psalm

O that today you would listen to his voice! Harden not your hearts . . .

That call to listen becomes an urgent call to me too. Today, this hour, this moment, I should be alert, for I might miss something that is given to me, something addressed to the heart, to the innermost self. These days can become a means of reminding me of what should be there all the time—a listening, hearing and responding to that continuous conversation, that speaking with God, that easy and natural meeting of two persons with one another in dialogue. Listen is the opening word of the Rule of St Benedict, the Rule by which Merton lived. If I am also to be true to my calling, my vocation, I must go on listening for this voice. There is such a danger that I talk about God, and enjoy talking about God, and do not stop and in the silence of my heart listen to Him speaking.

> The reality that is present to us and in us:
> call it Being . . . Silence.
> And the simple fact that by being attentive,
> by learning to listen
> (or recovering the natural capacity to listen)
> we can find ourself engulfed in such happiness
> that it cannot be explained:
> the happiness of being at one with everything
> in that hidden ground of Love
> for which there can be no explanations.
> . . .
> May we all grow in grace and peace,
> and not neglect the silence that is printed
> in the centre of our being.
> It will not fail us.
> It is more than silence.
> Jesus spoke of the spring of living water, you remember
> . . .

> Alleluia!
> I love the Lord for he has heard
> the cry of my appeal;
> for he turned his ear to me
> in the day when I called him.

How gracious is the Lord, and just;
our God has compassion.
The Lord protects the simple hearts;
I was helpless so he saved me.

Turn back, my soul, to your rest
for the Lord has been good;
he has kept my soul from death,
(my eyes from tears)
and my feet from stumbling.

I will walk in the presence of the Lord
in the land of the living.
(Psalm 114 [116], verses 1, 2, 5-9)

DAY TWO

Response

As I start to spend time with myself in silence before the Word, the Creator who made, loved, forgave and redeemed me, I also start to come face to face with my own weaknesses and failures, the darkness inside, the sense of sin. But Merton meets me here for this is something which he also met and faced.

> All of us who are called to a serious way of life are called
> to face the blackness of ourselves and of our world.
> If we have to live the victory of the Risen Christ over
> death we have to pass through death.
> Or arise out of our own death.
> It means seeing death and hell in ourselves.
> I never imagined when I was a novice and when "His
> lamp shone over my head" what it would mean to suffer
> the darkness which He Himself suffers in me.

Merton wrote this in a letter which he ends by referring to a very remarkable Russian monk who died in 1938, Staretz Silouan, a humble, outwardly ordinary man who identified himself with people in their sorrows and troubles, and whose compassion for them was an element of his interior silence. In his inner conflicts and sorrows he found a strange answer and a still stranger way of prayer.

The Lord said to him: "Keep thy soul in hell and despair not." At first it sounds a bit dreadful, or perhaps at best eccentric. Yet to me it is in a strange way comforting. Men still share deeply and silently the anguish of Christ abandoned by his Father (to be abandoned by God is to be "in hell") and they "despair not." How much better and saner it is to face despair and not to give in than to work away at keeping up appearances and patching up our conviction that a bogus spirituality is real! that we are not really facing dread! that we are all triumphantly advancing, "getting somewhere" (where?), accomplishing great things for Christ, and changing the face of the world.

As I stay with this passage, and pray with it, it allows me to recognise the conflict, sorrow, even despair within. I try not to disguise it—even from myself. This is a time for honesty, in which I need no longer keep up appearances. I can take off the mask, and stay with this naked self in such need of help. Merton's final words speak to me now:

> It takes courage
> But only then can I be found and saved by God.
>
> Let me be content with whatever darkness surrounds me,
> finding Him always by me, in His mercy.
>
> Save me, O God
> for the waters have risen to my neck.
>
> I have sunk into the mud of the deep
> and there is no foothold.
> I have entered the waters of the deep
> and the waves overwhelm me.

This is my prayer to you,
my prayer for your favour.
In your great love, answer me, O God,
with your help that never fails:
rescue me from sinking in the mud;
save me from my foes.
(Psalm 68 [69], verses, 2, 3, 14, 15)

"This is my prayer to you . . ." The psalmist speaks on my behalf, and on behalf of all the other suffering members of humanity.
Here we bring our own sin and sorrow, our personal struggles
and interior conflicts, and offer them up to God, not in our own
words but in the words of the psalms. And when we do this Merton
helps us to enter into the "action" of the psalm, allowing our own
sorrow and struggle to be swallowed up into a wider sorrow and
struggle, and so swept away on the strong tide of the psalmist's
ultimate hope that in the end God will save us.

To you all flesh will come
With its burden of sin
Too heavy for us our offences
But you wipe them away.
(Psalm 64 [65], verse 3)

This is a death in which we have found Him Who is the
Way, the Truth and the Life. We know that this darkness, which seems to annihilate us, is not the darkness
of death but, if such an expression can be understood,
the darkness of life . . . If the paradox may be allowed,
this frightful death is our first taste of glory.

Then we begin to discover that the night in which
we seem to be lost is the protection of the shadow of
God's wings. If God has brought us into this darkness

it is because He wishes to guard us with extreme care and tenderness, or, in the words of the psalm "like the apple of His eye."

In front of the cross I reflect on what it was that brought Christ to hang there, in acute suffering, at the end of a short life in which all His words and His actions have spoken of a God of love. But I cannot stop here, with a picture of a group of people on a Palestinian hillside two thousand years ago. The sin that rejected that Christ so full of love is still in today's world, is still in each one of us. Sin is the refusal of love, whether to give love or to receive it. This is nothing abstract or remote, from which I can distance myself. It is daily in my life. It is concrete, immediate, close at hand.

One of the most poignant moments in his autobiography comes when Merton recounts a childhood episode, the implications of which remained with him long afterwards. He paints a picture of his younger brother as he stands watching Merton and his friends playing their games in the woods, a small boy, vulnerable and unhappy, who refuses to go away even when they start throwing stones in his direction. "He cannot understand why this law of love is being so wildly and unjustly violated in his case." At this point I stop, and I now ask myself how often I too have rejected love, betrayed love—the love of God which comes to me through human encounter.

Many times it was like that. And in a sense, this terrible situation is the pattern and the prototype of all sin: the deliberate and formal will to reject disinterested love for us for the purely arbitrary reason that we simply do not want it. We will to separate ourselves from that love. We reject it entirely and absolutely, and will not acknowledge it simply because it does not please us to be loved. Perhaps the inner motive is that we all need love from others, and depend upon the charity

of others to carry on our own lives. And we refuse to
love. . . .

I am reminded of the prodigal son, and as I think again of
that story I can identify myself with him. He took a long, hard
look at himself and where his attitudes and actions had brought
him. He "entered into himself," not as some lengthy, narcissistic
navel-gazing exercise, for that would have been thoroughly inap-
propriate, but simply as a meditation on his condition which was
brief and to the point. When he realised the foolishness of what
he had done he turned and came home, and asked for forgiveness.
"I will arise and go to my father, and I will say to Him, Father, I
have sinned against heaven, and before you and am I no longer
worthy to be called your son" (Luke 15:18-19).

> The Fathers of the church saw that every one of us is
> more or less like the Prodigal, starving in a distant land,
> far from our Father's house. This is the common condi-
> tion of mankind exiled from God and from Paradise
> by an inordinate preoccupation with perishing things
> and by a constant inclination towards self-gratification
> and sin.

There is an ancient monastic concept known as compunction.
The word itself carries all sorts of resonances. It is the experience
of being touched or pierced *(punctio)* by the awareness of my true
state before God, so at its heart lies a sense of pain, of stinging, a
sensation of being pricked. It means also that I am stung into action, aroused from torpor and complacency, and now long to do
better. Here is something positive, feeling God's love drawing me
on to better things, calling me into a new future. I am touched,
overwhelmed by the love of a God who forgives me and in the face
of that love I long for compromise to cease and instead to respond

totally to this amazing love which forgives and frees. While I am being forced to face ultimate truths about myself I am also at the same time being brought face to face with a loving trust in the God who saves. Merton used to teach his novices at Gethsemani the significance of compunction, and it also applies to me now. My recognition of sin brings with it a sense of sorrow, but I need to make sure that this sorrow is not one that feeds on itself, for that will never liberate me and bring me back to God. The danger is that I still see the evil of sin in relation to *myself* rather than to God. This may be rooted in exaggerated self-pity, and perhaps it goes with cowardly recriminations against God and myself. Its result is to confine me within myself, with my own guilt. It is sterile for it brings me nowhere, does not lead me to real repentance, and thus to change. But I see now that what I need is *compunction* which is very different, for it grows from openness and from love.

Out of the depths I cry to you, O Lord!
Lord, hear my voice!
O let your ears be attentive
to the voice of my pleading.

If you, O Lord, should mark our guilt,
Lord, who would survive?
But with you is found forgiveness:
for this we revere you.

My soul is waiting for the Lord,
I count on his word,
My soul is longing for the Lord,
more than watchman for daybreak,
Let the watchman count on daybreak
and Israel on the Lord.

Because with the Lord there is mercy
and fullness of redemption.
(Psalm 129 [130])

∼

As I now express sorrow for my sins I find that what Merton tells me can become a guideline.

If I can presume that the Lord wishes to speak through me in any way, I would say He wants us all to know not to punish ourselves and not to be Satan to ourselves. Let us accuse no one, punish no one, accuse ourselves rightly of course, but not as Satan does; rather as the woman with the issue of blood, who "accused" herself by touching the hem of His garment in secret and with many, many tears, almost despairing and yet hoping tremendously. This alone is our joy.

By this act of repentance, of turning and so returning to Christ, I allow the warmth of Christ's love to break down the resistance, the coldness and the hardness of heart which has kept me apart from Him.

Who turns the rock into a pool
And flint into a spring of water.
(Psalm 113 [114], verse 8)

∼

As Merton points us to the psalms and the differing levels at which they carry meaning, not only do we find ourselves sharing our suffering with the whole people of God, but with Christ Himself. For he reminds us that it is also Christ who speaks, sings, suffers, triumphs in the psalms, and thereby awakens in us a new sense of life and of His life-giving power.

We find out that when we bring our own sorrows and desires and hopes and fears to God, and plunge them all into the sorrows and hopes of the mysterious One (that is to say Christ) who sings these psalms, a kind of transformation is effected. We have put all that we have—or rather all our poverty, all that we have not—into the hands of Christ. . . . We find that in His poverty our poverty becomes infinite riches; in His sufferings our defeats are transformed into victory, and His death becomes our everlasting life.

What has happened?

We have been transformed.

So this day ends with the knowledge that I am forgiven, that the God who might have punished has instead chosen to forgive. If that is so then the least that I can do is to forgive myself. "It is Christ Himself who has identified Himself with us and begs us to begin by having mercy on ourselves, not now for our own sake but for His! . . . His is a strange way of forgiveness: He identifies Himself with us and asks us, as it were, to begin by forgiving ourselves. . . . Then He gives us peace with ourselves—because we are at peace with Him."

Fear has been turned into fortitude.
Anguish has become joy, without somehow ceasing to
     be anguish
and we triumph over suffering
not by escaping it,
but by completely accepting it.
This is the only triumph,
because there is no victory in evasion.

The Lord is compassion and love,
slow to anger and rich in mercy.
His wrath will come to an end
he will not be angry for ever.
He does not treat us according to our sins
nor repay us according to our faults.

For as the heavens are high above the earth
so strong is his love for those who fear him.
As far as the east is from the west
so far does he remove our sins.
(Psalm 102 [103], verses 8-12)

DAY THREE

The Solitary Within: The True Self

"What can we gain by sailing to the moon if we are not able to cross the abyss that separates us from ourselves? For me to be a saint means to be myself, because the problem of sanctity and salvation is in fact the problem of finding out who I am and of discovering my true self." When Merton says this of himself he is also telling me something that I need to know about myself on the next step of the retreat. Before I can truly know God I must know myself, the person I am, the unique creation of a loving Creator Father. "What is made by God in His own image and likeness must necessarily be a great good, and therefore it follows that it is a real evil if we regard human nature as evil, if we ignore the good within ourselves." Our first task then is to know ourselves—to know the good that is in us, to know God's love for us, so that we may reply to Him with the love of our own hearts and love Him "without measure." Since it is in prayer that I best come to know myself, the naked, real self, I can hardly hope to run away from myself during this retreat. Nor would I really want to for I know that it is fundamentally important, indeed life-giving, for all of us.

Here Merton is inviting me to join him on a journey of identity. It is a journey into becoming human. To fail to make such a journey is a denial of life. My life, my peace, my fulfilment all depend upon it.

> Therefore there is only one problem on which all my existence, my peace and my happiness depend: to discover myself in discovering God. If I find Him I will find myself and if I find my true self I will find Him.

We all have a journey to make into that true self, the person God wants us to be, wills us to become, the man or woman made in His own image and likeness. It is a life-long journey, and I pray that this retreat may carry me one step further in this movement from the old to the new self, from the false to the true. It is a journey which Merton knew well. To enter a monastery was not an escape from inner pain and conflict—in fact he said that the monastic vocation did not lessen but intensified a struggle which is inescapable for any of us. Since it occupied so much of his thought he wrote about it often, and vividly, sometimes in words which are not immediately easy, and which we may find we have to come back to time and again if we are to reap their full meaning. But essentially he is simply seeking himself—or letting himself be discovered by God.

> God leaves me free to be whatever I like.
> I can be myself, or not, as I please.
> I am at liberty to be real, or to be unreal.
> I may be true or false, the choice is mine.
> I may wear now one mask and now another,
> and never, if I so desire, appear with my own true face.

To work out my own identity in God,
which the Bible calls "working out our salvation,"
    is a labour that requires sacrifice and anguish, risk and
        many tears.

I do not know clearly beforehand what the result of
        this work will be,
the secret of my full identity is hidden in Him. He alone
        can make me who I am,
or rather who I will be when at last I fully begin to be.

In the opening words of his autobiography Merton presents himself as someone with whom we can easily identify as he tells us how he finds himself at once caught up in contradictory coils. "Free by nature, in the image of God, I was nevertheless the prisoner of my own violence and my own selfishness. . . . loving God and yet hating Him, born to love Him, living instead in fear and hopeless self-contradictory hungers."

It is this tension between what he is and what he is called to be which strikes an answering chord in me, in all of us. For it is simply the choice between nonliving and living, between death and freedom, truth, salvation.

If I never become what I am meant to be,
but always remain what I am not,
I shall spend eternity contradicting myself
by being at once something and nothing,
a life that wants to live and is dead,
a death that wants to be dead
and cannot quite achieve its own death because it still
        has to exist.

∾

The inner split between the two selves continued to haunt Merton—the superficial self which is proud, rebellious and fallen, and the true deep and contemplative self which is reconciled and forgiven. It is a theme to which he will return time and again. We all have this choice. We can dedicate our lives to truth or to falsity, to good or to evil. "We can give our lives to God or to mammon His enemy. We can surrender to Him who is, or we can cast ourselves away with one who is not, who is only the shadow and the negation and the denial of what is."

> There is an irreducible opposition between the deep, transcendent self that awakens only in contemplation, and the superficial, external self which we commonly identify with the first person singular. We must remember that this superficial "I" is not our real self. It is our "individuality" and our "empirical self" but it is not truly the hidden and mysterious person in whom we subsist before the eyes of God. The "I" that works in the world, thinks about itself, observes its own reactions and talks about itself is not the true "I" that has been united to God in Christ. It is at best the vesture, the mask, the disguise of that mysterious and unknown "self" whom most of us never discover until we die.

I feel that Merton is here trying to help me to recover possession of my deepest self, the self that lies beneath the exterior and which can only be found in God and through God—God's work in me is to bring about the wholeness and the fulfilment for which I long. Can I ask God's grace to invade me so totally that that may actually come about?

> For it was you who created my being
> knit me together in my mother's womb.

I thank you for the wonder of my being,
for the wonders of all your creation.

Already you knew my soul,
my body held no secret from you
when I was being fashioned in secret
and moulded in the depths of the earth.

Your eyes saw all my actions,
they were all of them written in your book;
every one of my days was decreed
before one of them came into being.

O search me, God, and know my heart.
O test me and know my thoughts.
See that I follow not the wrong path
and lead me in the path of life eternal.
(Psalm 138 [139], verses 13-16, 23-24)

To be truly human we have to regain what was lost by the first
Adam. Adam and Eve stand in the garden, created by God to share
in His life, to be in direct, intimate and constant relationship with
Him and to find their fulfilment in faithful response to Him. Yet
by their disobedience, which sprang out of their own self-will, they
lost that chance, threw it away. As that chance was lost through
disobedience, so it is only through obedience that it can be re-
covered. This reminds me that while I desire to be *like* God, and
that that is a God-given desire which God himself has implanted
in me, I must beware of wanting to *be* God, like Adam and Eve.

Nourished as his life was by the Rule of St Benedict Merton
would know only too well that sentence in the opening section,
the Prologue, "The labour of obedience will bring you back to him
from whom you had drifted through the sloth of disobedience."
The word sloth is one that I appreciate for if I am honest I must
admit that my failures are as likely to lie as much in laziness, in
drift, in heedlessness as in anything more dramatic. Come to life

says St Benedict, choose life. The Lord in his love shows us the way of life. Let us set out on this way. This is the opportunity that we are offered, the chance that we are given. We are being challenged to say Yes now, today, not tomorrow. This is not something that we can postpone. There is such urgency here. Merton, being himself a man fully alive, would want to rescue us from a semi-conscious, torpid kind of existence, half alive and half awake compared with what could be "the real life of our deep selves."

A time of retreat such as this helps me to stand aside and take a look at what is happening in my life. It gives me the opportunity to recall myself, recover, return.

> I must return to Paradise.
> I must *recover* myself,
> salvage my dignity,
> recollect my lost wits,
> return to my true identity.

The secret of my true identity is hidden in the love and the mercy of God. It is that deepest self in which I stand naked before God's love and mercy. It can only be discovered, or uncovered, in God. It is above all solitude and prayer which help to strip me of the false self, the ego which masks my true identity. Standing naked before God I no longer need any such disguise, for I stand before the One who knows me through and through. This false self is a hungry self, needing to be fed by achievement, always looking for praise, greedy for adulation and acclaim. It is at the centre of all my striving for gain and satisfaction, whether material or spiritual. It has to be pandered to, cultivated, developed, satisfied. When Merton speaks of it as the "smoke self," the "evanescent self," or calls it "an imposter and a stranger," it helps me to see how essentially superficial it is. It must disappear, die, or at least become changed, transformed.

Indeed you love truth in the heart:
then in the secret of my heart teach me wisdom
O purify me, then I shall be clean;
O wash me, I shall be whiter than snow.

A pure heart create for me, O God,
put a steadfast spirit within me.
Do not cast me away from your presence,
nor deprive me of your holy spirit.
(Psalm 50 [51], verses 8, 9, 12, 13)

That purification can only be the work of God. I therefore hand myself over to Him, saying as I do so, "Father, not my will but yours." What Merton saw so clearly, and what he wants to show us, is that our fundamental relationship with God must be one of total dependency upon Him. So we make our starting point our need to "submit ourselves entirely to God in order to let him work with us" since "in life and death we depend entirely on Him."

∽

"Not to accept and love and do God's will, is to refuse the fulness of my existence."

But as I stay with this, and make it into a prayer for myself, I realise that it asks of me three things

to accept

to love

to do

This transformation, which is wrought in me by a merciful God, will never be possible until I desire it and work to find it with God and in God.

My response must be to open myself to being a partner with God, working with Him, co-operating with the God who is my Maker and my Redeemer. I find that it helps me to think of this in terms of stewardship, responsibility, accountability. What use am I making of the raw material that has been given to me? At one point Merton uses the image of wax waiting for a seal. Without that stamp upon me I have no special identity. My destiny is to be softened and prepared in this life, by God's will, to receive at death the seal of my own degree of likeness to God in Christ. Only heat and fire can soften and prepare the wax for the seal. Perhaps I may not be willing to melt in that fire. Perhaps I may choose to resist, I may prefer to stay hard and brittle. As I listen to Merton I take time to reflect on what this passage tells me about myself and my response to God at work in me.

> Souls are like wax waiting for a seal.
> The wax that has melted in God's will
> can easily receive the stamp of its identity,
> the truth of what it was meant to be.
> But the wax that is hard and dry and brittle
> and without love
> will not take the seal:
> for the seal, descending upon it,
> grinds it to powder.
> Therefore if you spend your life
> trying to escape from the heat of the fire
> that is meant to soften and prepare you to become your
> true self
> and if you try to keep your substance from melting in
> the fire
> as if your true identity were to be hard wax—
> the seal will fall upon you at last and crush you.
> You will not be able to take your own true name and
> countenance,
> and you will be destroyed by the event that was meant
> to be your fulfilment.

⁓

All this is only possible in and through Christ Himself, the second Adam. God's unbelievable generosity in sending His only Son into the world makes this return possible. The proud and rebellious journey of the first Adam, who is me and each one of us, is reversed by Christ the second Adam. We learn from Him *how* to make that journey. We learn from Him that it asks of us obedience—Christ's own obedience, an obedience which He carried through to death. Ultimately it asks that we become more and more Christ-like. So this day of the retreat ends with the prayer that I may discover that innermost self "that truly loves with the love and the spirit of Christ, this 'I' is Christ Himself living in us."

Preserve me, God, I take refuge in you.
I say to the Lord: "You are my God.
My happiness lies in you alone."

O Lord, it is you who are my portion and my cup;
it is you yourself who are my prize.
The lot marked out for me is my delight:
welcome indeed the heritage that falls to me!

You will show me the path of life,
the fullness of joy in your presence,
at your right hand happiness for ever.
(Psalm 15 [16], verses 1, 2, 5, 6, 11)

DAY FOUR

Encounter With Christ

Christ himself is the focal point on this fourth step which brings me to the central day of this retreat—for it is on the figure of Christ that everything else converges.

> Whatever I have written, I think it can all be reduced in the end to this one root truth: that God calls human persons to union with Himself and with one another in Christ.

Merton's great friend Dan Walsh, who delivered the homily at his funeral, spoke of what he personally regarded as his true greatness: that deep and abiding sense of God in Christ. What he then went on to say can become a prayerful reflection for me that I may also come to know what Merton experienced,

> that deep and abiding sense of God in Christ—
> and of God in man through Christ—
> of Christ in his Church—
> Christ in each one of us through the action of his
>   Holy Spirit

the Christ of God who in the spirit of his love lives in
the people of God
the Christ who is in us when we love and serve one
another in true brotherhood
when we realise that we are not our brother's keeper
but our brother's brother.

I remind myself of Merton's early encounter with Christ which
he describes so vividly in his autobiography and how then for the
first time in his life he really began to pray, praying not with lips
or intellect or imagination, but praying out of the very roots of his
life, his being. His expression of what that sight of Christ meant to
him reads like a confession of faith—one in which I can join, and
let it become the occasion for me to celebrate the place of Christ
in my own life.

It was there I first saw Him,
Whom I now serve as my God and my King,
and Who owns and rules my life.
It is the Christ of the Apocalypse,
the Christ of the Martyrs,
the Christ of the Fathers.
It is the Christ of St Paul and of St John,
and of St Augustine and St Jerome,
and all the Fathers—and of the Desert Fathers.
It is Christ God, Christ King.

This is the Christ of whom later on when he has entered the
monastery he will say

He is the whole meaning of our life,
the whole substance of our monastic life.

Nothing in the monastery makes sense if we forget this
    great central truth.
We come seeking truth
Christ said "I am the truth."
We come seeking life.
He is also the way, and the life.
We come seeking light.
He is "the light of the world."
We come seeking God.
In Him "dwells the fullness of the Godhead." (Col. 2:9)

~

In *The Sign of Jonas* when he writes of a moment in which he rediscovered Christ, "or perhaps discovered Him for the first time," he adds that this is something that is happening all the time. As I read this passage and transform it into my own prayer, I ask that I too may come to know more intimately and immediately this Christ who sees me wherever I am, and who sees me with love.

His eyes, which are the eyes of Truth, are fixed upon
    my heart.
Where His glance falls, there is peace;
for the light of His Face, which is the Truth, produces
    truth wherever it shines.
There too is joy:
And he says to those He loves—"I will fix my eyes upon
    thee."
His eyes are always on us in choir and everywhere and
    in all times.
No grace comes to us from heaven except He looks
    upon our hearts.

And what is more—He looks at us from within our
own hearts, for we and He are one.

This Christ who enters our hearts is someone whom we come
to know as friend.

Christ has granted us His Friendship
so that He may in this manner enter our hearts
and dwell in them as a personal presence,
not as an *object*, not as a "what" but as a "Who."

This He is who He is,
is present in the depths of our own being as our Friend,
and as our other self.

Without Christ
there would be no salvation,
no happiness,
no joy,
because we would be irrevocably cut off from God,
the source of all life and joy.
We must realise, above all,
how utterly useless is human effort to please God,
without Christ.
We cannot save ourselves,
no matter how heroic may be our sacrifices,
without Christ.

Here then is our situation—
without Christ we are entirely cut off from God,
we have no access to Him . . .
With and *in* Christ
all our lives are transformed and sanctified.

"We seek Christ Crucified as our redemption, as our
strength, our wisdom, our life in God" (1 Cor.
1:23-4).
We cannot fully understand this if we do not understand the love and compassion of Christ for us
in our weakness.
He is a loving Saviour
who has come down to our level
to give us His strength.

The meditation on the power of Christ continues as Merton
now leads us more deeply into a rediscovery, a recognition of the
Christ in the Trinity and in each one of us.

Christianity is life and wisdom in Christ,
It is a return to the Father in Christ.
It is a return to the infinite abyss of pure reality in
which our own reality is grounded
and in which we exist.
It is a return to the source of all meaning and all truth.

It is a rediscovery of paradise within our own spirit, by
self-forgetfulness.
And, because of our oneness with Christ,
It is the recognition of ourselves as sons and daughters
of the Father.
It is the recognition of ourselves as other Christs.
It is the awareness of strength and love imparted to us
by the miraculous presence of the Nameless and
Hidden One Whom we call the Holy Spirit.

But then as well as these great hymns of celebration of the power of Christ there is also the encounter with the hidden Christ. The idea of Christ coming as the tiny child, secret, hidden within us, was popular among the twelfth-century Cistercians as they contemplated the mercy of God in the mystery of Christ's birth. "Our Christ-life is a gift of the infinite mercy of God." We have been given this free gift of love, and we must receive it with free and grateful love. Otherwise it cannot be received at all. Merton is here reflecting on the Christmas sermons of Guerric of Igny, on this theme, the gift of love, the merciful love of God, and how we respond to that gift. Christ has been given to us to make our salvation easy and joyful, "and if we will only look at Him, and see the greatness of God's mercy radiating from the gift of the Incarnate Word, we will be unable to resist His love, unable to remain cold, despondent and sad. We will respond to His gift of Himself with the spontaneous gift of our own selves . . ."

The child lying there in the manger is the little Word, given to us to be cherished and nurtured. Guerric is here telling all of us of our own "motherhood" of Christ, showing us how we should receive this new-born infant with gentle solicitude and maternal care. So he is reminding me of the grace and the demands of being a mother, the qualities of gentleness and tenderness that it asks of me, the readiness to nurture and to foster growth. These are qualities which he says belong both to each one of us individually and also to the community as a whole. It is good to take time to reflect prayerfully on the responsibility of this gift.

> Guard it, nurture it tenderly, as the Infant Christ, until the Child Who was born for you may be formed in you. He, not only by being born but by living and dying, has handed over to us the pattern which we must follow. He needed not to be born for Himself, or to live or die for Himself. He was born, lived and died only for us that we might be born through Him, live according to Him, and die in Him, who lives and abides for ever.

~

Another twelfth-century Cistercian, Isaac of Stella, carries the image further when he speaks of the *growth* of this child in our hearts. Blessed, he tells us, is the soul that never forgets or lets go of the child Jesus. But then he goes on to say that we must also contemplate the grown Jesus. Just as the son of Abraham became very great, and as that son was Isaac whose name means laughter, so "let the Son of God grow in thee, for He is formed in thee, and from thee, and may He become to thee a great smile and exultation and perfect joy which no man can take from thee."

Merton's own time of private prayer remains secret—though the way in which his whole being radiated "a great smile and exultation" must surely tell us a great deal. It is in fact most often in his letters that we can glimpse the Merton of prayer, for here, to friends and enquirers he was rather less reticent about his own hidden spiritual life. Writing to the great Zen scholar Daisetz Suzuki he speaks of the Christ within.

The Christ we seek is within us,
in our inmost self,
is our inmost self,
and yet infinitely transcends ourselves.

Christ himself is in us as unknown and unseen.
We follow Him,
we find Him,
and then He must vanish,
and we must go along without Him at our side.
Why?
Because He is even closer than that.
He is *ourself*.

It is in the very depths of my being that Christ dwells. That thought is fundamental to Merton. In one of his last conferences in India on his final journey, he spoke most movingly of how in our lives, lives of faithful love, we must reveal this great mystery of God's love for us. As I read this I try to deepen my commitment to that same faithful love in my own life.

> This is the very root of our being.
> Therefore what we are called to do
> is to live as habitually and constantly as possible
> with great simplicity
> on this level of love
> which proceeds from the depths of our own being
> where Christ reigns and loves.
> This is a dimension of love which no one can take away
> unless we close the door ourselves
> and no one can bring it in
> unless we open the door to Christ
> opening our hearts to Christ
> and dwelling there.

~

But the Christ child in our hearts is also the Christ crucified on the cross. As we come closer and closer to the mystery of the love of Christ we are drawn to see the depths of that love in the figure who holds out His arms to all of us from the cross, and whose suffering is the most eloquent expression of that love. Any authentic following of Christ is a movement into the obscurity, the loneliness and the sorrow of the Christ on Calvary. So the heart of Christ within me opens up to me that most mysterious part of myself which Merton could only describe as "le point vierge": the inmost desire in the heart of Christ makes itself somehow present in us in the form of that little point of nothingness and poverty in us which is the "point" or virgin eye by which we know Him.

We do not need to *know* and to *understand* about the cross and the way to the kingdom,

> What we need to know
> is the inmost desire in the heart of Christ,
> which is that we should come to the Kingdom with Him.
> He alone knows the way,
> which is that of the cross.

It is in Christ that I find myself restored, made whole and made free. What do I do in response to Christ in my life? That is the question which faces me at this point in the retreat, for that is where everything else is focused. Surrender to Christ: so easy to say. But can I actually do it now? Lay at His feet the whole of myself, the self that is hurt and wounded, my joyous and smiling self, and simply ask Him to grow in my heart.

> The Lord is my light and my help;
> whom shall I fear?
> The Lord is the stronghold of my life;
> before whom shall I shrink?
>
> There is one thing I ask of the Lord,
> for this I long,
> to live in the house of the Lord,
> all the days of my life.
>
> O Lord, hear my voice when I call;
> have mercy and answer.
> Of you my heart has spoken:
> "Seek his face."
> *(Psalm 26 [27], verses 1, 4, 7, 8)*

DAY FIVE

The Demands of Love

The encounter with Christ in love must be followed by the encounter with other people in and through that same love. The one leads naturally to the other for the two are really inseparable. This brings me therefore to the next step of the retreat. If I have come to know Christ in my life then I also come to know "Christ in each one of us through the action of his Holy Spirit, the Christ who is in us when we love and serve one another."

If there is one constant theme in Merton's life and writing it is that he was living the solitary life not in order to escape from others but in order to find them in God. He was very much aware of his friends, his brothers and sisters, and how they should be loved.

If I allow Christ to use my heart in order to love my
brothers and sisters with it,
I will soon find that Christ loving in me and through
me has brought to light Christ in my brothers
and sisters.
And I will find that the love of Christ in my brothers,
and sisters, loving me in return,
has drawn forth the image and the reality of Christ in
my own soul.

If I believe in a God who takes on the human form and enters into a human body then I need to think out the implications of that in the way in which I regard other people. "Since the Word was made Flesh, God is in man, God is in *all men.*" If I fail to see this, and to act on it, however difficult and costly that may be, Merton tells me that I am being disloyal to one of the most basic truths of my faith.

> All men and women are to be seen and treated as Christ. Failure to do this, the Lord tells us, involves condemnation for disloyalty to the most fundamental of revealed truths. "I was thirsty and you gave me not to drink. I was hungry and you gave me not to eat . . ." (Matt 25:24). This could be extended all over the entire area of human needs, not only for bread, for work, for liberty, for health, but also for truth, for belief, for love, for acceptance, for fellowship and understanding.

But the ability, or the gift, of being able to love others fully and truly, as they need to be loved, depends on my own self, on the true self whom I was trying to uncover on the third step of the journey. It also depends on the solitude which I explored on the first day of the retreat. There is a helpful image about how in solitude I am able to draw closer to those I love which comes in something written about Merton by one of his former novices. He asks us to imagine a large group of people formed into a circle. As each individual in the circle begins to walk slowly towards the centre of the circle he or she finds that all are inevitably drawing closer to one another. It is of course physically impossible for them all to stand in the precise centre. But in prayer this can become possible, for Christ is that centre. As we go out of ourselves to Him in solitary prayer we go out of ourselves into the most real dimension of others—not the changing and shifting self, but rather the true self, the self that is grounded in the love of Christ.

Here I am being shown a love which, because it springs from the depths of my own inner centre, allows me to reach out to others in their own centre—and that is true communion. Often our love for others is not love at all, but only the need to be sustained in our illusions, even as we sustain others in theirs. Merton writes about this very clearly and honestly, and I need to hear what he is telling me, for it comes out of his own prayerful reflection and his lived out experience. Only when we have renounced these illusions can we then go out to others in true compassion. "It is in solitude that illusions finally dissolve. . . . He who is truly alone truly finds in himself the heart of compassion with which to love not only this man or that, but all men. He sees them all in the One who is the Word of God, the perfect manifestation of God's love, Jesus Christ."

The love that Merton is showing me here is a freeing love, not a love that wants to possess or to manipulate the other. For if I see in each person the presence of Christ (which must remain ultimately mystery), then that asks of me to respect the mystery that each one is.

> If we believe in the Incarnation of the Son of God,
> there should be no one on earth
> in whom we are not prepared to see,
> in mystery,
> the presence of Christ.

~

If I say that I am precious in God's sight—because of *His* goodness, not my own, I am saying something about my own worth. If I do not fulfil my destiny, becoming the person made in His own image and likeness that He wants me to be, His mercy is frustrated. My whole being, my life, my actions, become valuable in proportion as I love God and as I desire His will to be worked out in me. Merton says, "We must be meek and loving, even towards ourselves, especially towards ourselves." I now make this into a prayer for myself. I do not pray it lightly as I look into the very depths of the darkness within, and stay with all the painful, wounded, sinful parts of myself, offering them up as part of the prayer. Merton is speaking of this love that we have for ourselves as, and because of, God's love for us.

> This too I have learned or begun to learn in hell.
> Oh, the mercy of God.
> We are its ministers, even for ourselves.
> We must minister mercy to our hateful self, and to our
>   brother in whom we must see our own condition
>   reflected.
> Thus we become Christs, in no other way can we.

Here I am being given a description of pure love. It is wonderfully freeing. If it makes me so totally certain of myself, of my own dignity and my own lovableness for the best and highest of reasons, then I no longer need to make demands on my brothers and sisters to prove anything to myself, turning to them to make up the lacunae and inadequacies within myself. I try to see what it means if I am to love my brothers and sisters as God would have me do from such a confident and assured base. For it is only as I find this freedom within myself that I can afford to relax my grasp on others, since I now no longer need their dependence.

I find myself brought back to the theme of the mystery that each one of us is.

> A person is a person insofar as each has a secret
> and is a solitude of their own
>   that cannot be communicated to anyone else.

I will love that which most makes them a person:
the secrecy,
the hiddenness,
the solitude of their own individual being,
which God alone can penetrate and understand.

A love that breaks into the spiritual privacy of another
in order to lay open all their secrets
and besiege their solitude with importunity,
does not love them:
it seeks to destroy what is best in them,
and what is most intimately theirs.

It is for this reason that Merton warns us, in a nicely chosen phrase, that we are not expected to be "a kind of radio-electric eye which is meant to assess the state of our neighbours' conscience." We are not there to see whether or not our neighbour is Christ, but to *recognise* Christ in them and to help our love make both them and us more fully alive in Christ. It is precisely this beauty and this dignity, this core of reality, the person that we each are in God's eyes, which we must respect in the other. He sees us all as linked together in Christ, and gives us a telling image of the needle and thread to express what that means. "It is the needle by which we draw the thread of charity through our neighbour's soul and our own soul and sew ourselves together in one Christ."

On one of his rare visits to the neighbouring town of Louisville, Merton stood on the pavement at the corner of the street and looked with love at all these people whom he did not know. He looked at them with a Christ love that saw in them a beauty and a dignity of which they themselves were probably totally unaware.

In Louisville, at the corner of Fourth and Walnut, in
the center of the shopping district, I was suddenly
overwhelmed with the realisation that I loved all those

people, that they were mine and I theirs, that we could not be alien to one another even though we were total strangers . . . Then it was as though I suddenly saw the secret beauty of their hearts, the depths of their hearts where neither sin nor desire nor self-knowledge can reach, the core of their reality, the person that each one is in God's eyes. If only they could see themselves as they really *are*.

Reading this I find that I catch Merton's own energy and enjoyment, his immense sense of joy at being human, at being part of the whole human race. It makes me reflect on how easily and how frequently I take my own humanity for granted.

It is a glorious destiny to be a member of the human race, though it is a race dedicated to many absurdities and one which makes many terrible mistakes: yet, with all that, God Himself gloried in becoming a member of the human race. A member of the human race! To think that such a commonplace realisation should suddenly seem like news that one holds the winning ticket in a cosmic sweepstake.

I have the immense joy of being man, a member of a race in which God Himself became incarnate. As if the sorrows and stupidities of the human condition could overwhelm me, now I realise what we all are. There is no way of telling people that they are all walking around shining like the sun . . .

⁓

This celebration of love, and rejoicing in love, is never facile, easy-going love. It is a love patterned on Christ's own example, the love of Christ himself, the good shepherd, the teacher, the healer, the suffering servant. Talking on the passion to the novices at Gethsemani Merton painted a picture of Christ during his last week on earth. It is by this standard that we should measure ourselves. We see a love without weakness, even in the midst of fear; without selfishness, even in the face of such unfair treatment; without anxiety even in the midst of persecution; and then finally, on the cross itself, the greatest example of Christ's love, the ability to forgive. Merton has moved a long way since his first encounter with Christ in Rome. He has come to know the Christ who is the suffering servant, who continues to love through betrayal, rejection, and pain. It is with this figure of Christ on the cross in mind that I think of two sentences in which Merton speaks of love as a mending of broken bones. I remember finding them on a memorial to him at New Harmony in Indiana and copying them down for what they said to me of the costliness of love. Merton was writing out of experience of the demands of love in a monastic community, but most of us live in a community of some sort, whether in family or marriage, parish, school or office, and what he says is equally true for us.

As long as we are on earth the love that unites us will bring us suffering by our very contact with one another. Because of this, love is the resetting of a body of broken bones. Even saints cannot live with saints on this earth without some anguish, without some pain at the differences that come between them.

O Lord how precious is your love.

Keep on loving those who know you.
(Lines from Psalm 35 [36], verses 7 and 10)

I thank you for your faithfulness and love,
Which excel all we ever knew of you.

You stretch out your hand and save me,
Your hand will do all things for me,
Your love O Lord is eternal,
Discard not the work of your hands.
(Psalm 137 [138], verses 2, 7)

DAY SIX

"Common and Natural and Ordinary"

If this retreat encourages me to spend time in prayful reflection on the people in my life it should also help me in my relationships with the material things of the world in which I live and work. As this time of solitude begins to come to an end I become increasingly aware that my calling places me in very ordinary daily circumstances where I need to find God. I pray that the time that I shall spend today may help me towards an awareness of God present in and through the world of His creating. By His incarnation, by His coming to us in ordinary human flesh, our God did not repudiate or reject the world which He had made and now entered in the form of a tiny child. "I will not take you out of the world" has implications that I need to take seriously. If I am searching for the Jesus who is the Word made flesh then I must see all material things in the light of the mystery of the incarnation, and I must reverence all creation because that Word became flesh. In his autobiography Merton had said, "all our salvation begins on the level of common and natural and ordinary things." I see that as a key to the whole of his journey. In all his writing he points us to the right places in which to look for God, and shows us that those places are there in front of us, right where we are. But we need to learn to see, to hear and to feel. At one point he speaks of "spiritual wonder." He reminds me of what I really know but need to rediscover time and again (and this retreat brings me that opportunity)—"spontaneous awe at the sacredness of life." Merton once used the phrase "an unspeakable reverence for the holiness of created things," and I shall take that as the text for this stage of the retreat.

Created things played a large part in his life. He loved people but he also loved nature. He tells us to begin "by learning *how to see and respect the visible creation* which mirrors the glory and the perfection of the invisible God." Already as a small child growing up in France he was able to receive "actual grace out of the sacrament of the land, and to contemplate God," even if at the time he did not fully realise it. In later life he easily found God in nature, and there are many places where he catches the light and colour and sound around him, and finds that they lead him to God.

> Halfway down, and in a place of comparative shelter, just before the pine trees begin, I found a bower God had prepared for me. It had been designed especially for this moment. There was a tree stump, in an even place. It was dry and a small cedar arched over it, like a green tent, forming an alcove. There I sat in silence and loved the wind in the forest and listened for a good while to God.

In moments such as these he felt himself to be particularly open, alive in all of his senses. On one occasion he describes how intensely he sees the world, how his renewal by the Word is paralleled by nature.

> By the reading of Scripture I am so renewed that all nature seems renewed around me and with me. The sky

seems to be a purer, a cooler blue, the trees a deeper green, light is sharper on the outlines of the forests and the hills and the whole world is charged with the glory of God and I feel fire and music in the earth under my feet.

~

When he visited the sisters at Our Lady of the Redwoods in California on his way to Bangkok, he found an atmosphere of deep prayer in their chapel with its one window opening out into a small clearing in the forest. "Enjoy this," he said. "Drink it all in. Everything, the redwood forests, the sea, the sky, the waves, the birds, the sea-lions. It is in all this that you will find your answers. Here is where everything connects." He is in effect telling us that we must start where we are, wherever we may find ourselves on the face of the earth. My difficulty comes in the fact that I neglect this, that I fail to see it, perhaps simply because I do not take enough time. Yet Merton is insistent that we live in the fullness of time, that we don't have to rush after it, that what we seek is already there and if we give it time it will make itself known to us. This was something that his life in the hermitage taught him.

> One of the best things for me when I went to the hermitage was being attentive to the times of the day: when the birds began to sing, and the deer came out of the morning fog, and the sun came up . . . The reason why we don't take time is a feeling that we have to keep moving. This is a real sickness. Today time is a commodity, and for each one of us time is mortgaged . . . we are threatened by a chain reaction: overwork—overstimulation—overcompensation—overkill.

There is an acute awareness in the monastic life with its daily, weekly, yearly rhythms of the changing pattern of time and season, light and dark. This is marked both by the readings in worship and by the hymns, many of them very ancient. This hymn for example which would be sung at Lauds, at daybreak, comes from the fifth century.

> The night, the darkness and its mist
> Have wrapped the world in heavy clouds,
> They take to flight as light returns,
> And Christ comes now to bless the day.

An evening hymn, attributed to St Gregory the Great, in the sixth century is a celebration of creation.

> O God you formed the elements
> The waters, fire, the earth and air,
> Assigning each their work and place
> That they may praise you everywhere.

Merton's day in the hermitage marked time and season, light and dark. It opened with rituals of its own. He would rise at 2:15 a.m. when the night was at its darkest and most silent.

> It is necessary for me to see the first point of light which begins to dawn. It is necessary to be present alone at the resurrection of Day, in blank silence when the sun appears. In this completely neutral instant I receive from the eastern woods, the tall oaks, the one word "Day" which is never the same. It is never spoken in any known language.

Rituals. Washing out the coffee pot in the rain bucket. Approaching the outhouse with circumspection on account of the king snake who likes to curl up on one of the beams inside. Addressing the possible king snake in the outhouse and informing him that he should not be there. Asking the formal ritual question that is asked at this time every morning: "Are you in there?"

More rituals: Spray bedroom (cockroaches and mosquitoes). Close all the windows on south side (heat). Leave windows open on north and east sides (cool). Leave windows open on west side until maybe June when it gets very hot on all sides. Pull down shades. Get water bottle. Rosary. Watch. Library book to be returned.

It is time to visit the human race.

When John Howard Griffin was living in the hermitage, to work on Merton's papers after his death, he kept to Merton's timetable and in his journal tells how this brought him close to the way in which Merton had used his time for prayer. The hours before dawn were the time of his secret prayer. This was above all when he prayed the psalms. But his way of praying took up everything that came to hand, those other things which as Howard Griffin lists them, I try to find parallels for in my own life.

. . . the psalms of the rain,
of the odors and crackling of the fire,
the psalms of the stars and the clouds and the winds
     in the trees—
all equally eloquent.
And also in this context,
the psalms of one's coughings and sneezings and coffee
     drinkings.

The psalms of one's heat rash—
for in this nothing need be hidden from God,
and nothing is lower than any other thing.
All things are taken up and become whole in
contemplation.
One does not waste time sorting them, grading them,
    evaluating them.
They are there as reality, and that is that.
They do not offend God.

Often in my own life I lose sight of the fact "that even the most ordinary actions of our everyday life are invested, by their nature, with a deep spiritual meaning." But Merton never forgot this. The monastic life takes the ordinary, the mundane, the humdrum, and makes that a way to God. We find in the Rule of St Benedict that the monk is told to handle the humblest material things with reverence and respect. The garden tools or the pots and pans in kitchen or pantry are to be treated with just as much care as the sacred vessels of the altar. Merton writes of how the monk comes to love his monastery and to find it "the house of God and the gate of Heaven." Buildings, furniture, farming equipment are all respected, valued and even loved, not for their own sakes but for the sake of God to whom they belong.

Religion in Wood is the title of a book of photographs of Shaker furniture for which Merton wrote the introduction. He found in these dissenting communities, which had come to America from England in the eighteenth century, a people dedicated to working with their hands, who made their work into prayer. Each piece of work that they undertook was work that was done patiently, gently, lovingly, so that it became in effect an act of worship. "The craftsman began each new chair as if it were the first chair ever to be made in the world." Their craftsmanship was a reflection of their love of God. Each thing had to fulfil its own vocation, to be precisely what it was supposed to be. The carpenter or cabinet maker was simply enabling the wood to respond to the "call" to become a chair, a table, a chest. "One feels that for the Shaker craftsman love of God and love of truth in one's own work came to the same thing, and work itself was a prayer, a communion with the inmost spiritual reality of things and so with God . . ." The work of their hands was therefore an expression of love, of "tenderness and care for all living beings, and indeed for life itself."

~

In Merton I see a man who is totally present to whatever he is doing, whatever he is handling. He takes the simplest realities of life, gives them time, allows them to be themselves, allows them to reveal God. This is something that I want to learn, discover for myself, and take from this retreat into my daily life. I ask God to help me to see, to touch, to be aware. This is why I am so grateful for Merton's photographs, for they allow me to see through his eyes, and I see his gentleness, his respect, his reverence for the worth of each thing however simple. His photography expresses just what he so much revered in his father's painting, a vision of the world that was without decoration or superfluous comment, "full of balance, full of veneration for structure, for the relation of masses and for all the circumstances that impress an individual identity on each created thing." He did not, as Howard Griffin tells us "seek to capture or possess . . . he allowed the objects to remain true to themselves and to reveal themselves."

Finding this love and joy in created things asks of me detachment. Just as with people, I do not own or possess. Everything is mystery. I thank God for his amazing generosity and as I do so I pray that I may grow in awareness, in detachment, in gratitude.

As soon as we take them to ourselves,
appropriate them,
hug them to our hearts,
we have stolen them from God,
they are no longer His, but our own.

They say to us:
"You can use me, and God our Father created me that
     I might be used by you.
I am His messenger sent to tell you the way to
Him. . . .
If you respect me, and leave me as I am,
and do not seek to seize me with a full and selfish
possession
then I will bring you joy:
for I will remain what I am."

You stretch out the heavens like a tent,
Above the rains you build your dwelling.
You make the clouds your chariot,
you walk on the wings of the wind.
You make the winds your messengers
and flashing fire your servants . . .

How many are your works, O Lord!
In wisdom you made them all,
The earth is full of your riches.
(Psalm 103 [104], verses 2, 3, 4, 24)

DAY SEVEN

Integration

Each of us has to find the unity in which everything
    fits and takes its right place
Each must work out just what the right amount may be.
And it varies at different times of our life.

Merton's search for unity was a life-long search. As this retreat comes to its end that also becomes my own task: the holding together of all those elements in my life that will bring me energy and integration. I know only too well what it is like to live as a distracted person, pulled first in one direction and then in another, and one of the purposes of this time apart has been to have the chance to think before God about the person I am now, my place in God's world, and the direction in which my life points me. Above all I need to decide how I can hold together my life of inner stillness and prayer, the contemplative side of myself, the Mary, with the Martha who is committed to the demands of a busy active life.

Merton is such a good guide here for he was so aware of being pulled in many directions. His journey was never tranquil for he was always facing up to tensions within himself, and in the outside world. Even when he was still quite young he was always conscious of the "tremendous immanent powers of light or darkness, peace or conflict, order or confusion, love or sin." The choices are open;

the question faces me, as it faced Merton, faces each one of us. In which direction shall we go?

~

Merton was prepared to face questions with honesty and without evasion. All his life he was moving forward, being drawn by new ventures and new issues. He struggled with conflict, and when in the 1950s and 60s he became involved in peace issues it was as though the outer world mirrored his inner reality. He knew that peace in the world can only exist if each of us is at peace in the core of our being. As he watched the forces of hate and anger, of violence and destruction, and saw the pain and fragmentation that resulted, he wrote about the human need for harmony, for a whole and integrated experience of peace at all levels, physical, emotional and spiritual, both individual and communal.

One way of seeing Merton's life is as "an odyssey towards unity." His path towards healing and maturity was one of unification. He faced the opposites and the tensions within himself, and let them converge. In doing this he becomes a symbol of the way in which we have watched in the twentieth century the bringing together of East and West, of masculine and feminine, secular and religious. "We must contain all divided worlds in ourselves," he once said. He learnt much in his later years from the study of Eastern thought and in particular from Zen. He spent five years studying texts from fourth and fifth century Taoist circles. He was attracted to them because he found there "a certain taste for simplicity, for humility, self-effacement, silence and in general a refusal to take seriously the aggressivity, the ambition, the push, the self-importance which one must display in order to get along in society." He also discovered here the role played by the central pivot through which passed Yes and No, I and non-I. Here he found the complementarity of opposites, and this became extremely important for him.

We see it in the yin-yang symbol.

Here then are light/dark, good/evil, masculine/feminine. The white and the black show that contradiction exists, and yet each flows into the other. At the start of each there is a small portion of the other. Taken separately each side appears contradictory; taken as a whole they flow together and become one dynamic unity.

∾

Perhaps the biggest contradiction for Merton, as for so many of us, was the holding together of a life of prayer with a life of activity so that the one may flow smoothly into the other, and the two can be held together as a dynamic unity. This is where he is so relevant for me on this final day of the retreat. How do I combine both Mary and Martha? How do I work out a commitment to time for silence and for prayer and a commitment to doing my job properly and my responsibilities towards the people who need me? This is a question about which Merton thought and wrote a great deal throughout his life. The hermitage did not take him away from the urgent needs and demands of the world. Rather it brought him closer to the world's problems and he addressed those problems out of a heart of compassion which came to him through his prayer.

True solitude is deeply aware of the world's needs.
It does not hold the world at arm's length.

> It is in deep solitude
> that I find the gentleness
> with which I can truly love my brothers and my
>   sisters.

> The more solitary I am,
> the more affection I have for them.

> It is pure affection,
> and filled with reverence
> for the solitude of others.
> Solitude and silence
> teach me to love my brothers and my sisters
> for what they are,
> not for what they say.

It might seem ironic that prayer in solitude should bring a deeper awareness of the world's needs. Yet this is what Merton is telling us time and again. He would say that any question of choosing the world or choosing Christ, as though deciding between two conflicting realities, was completely misguided.

> Do we choose Christ by choosing the world as it really
> is in him, that is to say created and redeemed by him,
> and encountered in the ground of our own personal
> freedom and of our love?

> . . .

> If the deepest ground of my being is love, then in that
> very love itself and nowhere else will I find myself, and
> the world, and my brother and Christ.

It is not a question of either-or but of all-in-one . . .
of wholeness, wholeheartedness and unity . . . which
finds the same ground of love in everything.

∼

Merton is insisting that it is a mistake to separate the life of
contemplative prayer and the life of ordinary daily work in the
world. He would not say that one is superior to the other. He was
quite clear that those involved in active social protest organisations
needed time for silence and solitude and inner quiet, that this was
a necessity and not a luxury. He said that "silence and the unclut-
tering of the mind" was even more important for social activists
living in the world than for monks in their cloisters. Knowing the
sort of momentum that this kind of activity can easily encourage
he warned, "Inside of yourselves, you shouldn't be running all the
time," and said how imperative it was to "protect the spirit from
ambushes of busyness and schedules."

His use of that word "ambush" startles me. It strikes home. Perhaps at this stage of the retreat I should stop, and face as honestly
and clearly as I can the snares and traps which lie in ambush in
the days ahead, which could so quickly enmesh me again. I have
so many things competing for my attention, and there is often a
temptation to be very busy. It seems almost inevitable that I find
myself caught up in far too much busyness, too much rushing
about, too much frenetic activity. And yet I also know that it need
not really be like this. The first step in making some sort of change,
however small and undramatic, must come from the conviction
that prayer, silence and solitude are the most important priorities
in my life. I need to decide how I can give them the attention, the
time and space that they deserve. There is nothing for it but to be
entirely practical about this. I must now work out my commit-
ments, look at the pattern of my day, and see if it can be changed.

The actual length of time for prayer is ultimately not so important as the faithfulness and discipline that it will ask of me. These will be my offerings to God at the end of this retreat. But I want to do this as Merton does in a spirit of love, of rejoicing in my own humanity and rejoicing in God's world. I think of the sense that he brings me of fullness of life. I think of how he says that it is all given, that "every moment is God's good time . . . We don't have to rush after it. It is there all the time."

∽

These days began with a call, and they must end with a call, for *today* I must hear His voice and must not harden my heart. That call awakens me to the fact that every minute, every moment can be spent in the presence of God, alive, aware of His love.

> We must learn to realise
> that the love of God sees us in every situation,
> and seeks our good.
> His inscrutable love seeks our awakening.

I am awakened to "the possibility of an uninterrupted dialogue with God." A dialogue of love is a response of my own free choice. That love is reaching out to the true self, not the self that is trapped in illusion and false expectations. So now I pray that I may once again ask God to set me free to yield myself up to that love that awaits me.

> God cannot plant his liberty in me
> because I am a prisoner
> and I do not even desire to be free.
> . . .

I must learn to "leave myself"
in order to find myself
by yielding to the love of God.

It was that love that I was thinking about on day six as I realised
how all things in creation are the signs of God's generosity.

For it is God's love that warms me in the sun and God's
love that sends the cold rain.
It is God's love that feeds me in the bread I eat and God
that feeds me also by hunger and fasting
It is the love of God that sends the winter days when I
am cold and sick,
and the hot summer when I labour and my clothes are
full of sweat:
but it is God Who breathes on me with the light winds
off the river
and in the breezes out of the wood.

～

If I were to stop rushing after things, or running inside myself, then I might be more able to think, walking with God in the
world of His creating, rejoicing in His love and His generosity.
Or perhaps instead of walking I should allow myself to think of
dancing. One of the most lyrical and poetic passages that Merton
ever wrote is the last chapter of *New Seeds of Contemplation*, called
"The General Dance." It is a wonderful piece of writing to bring this
retreat to its conclusion, for it draws together so much that I have
been thinking and praying about, during this time with Merton. It
is an invitation to become part of that dance, in harmony with the
whole universe, with my fellow-human beings, with the totality of

all creation. Here is God who wants to draw me away from life's illusions so that I can discover my true self in Him.

Merton tells me that this great cosmic dance is going on all the time, and I am in the midst of it whether I recognise it or not. It is only when I have the stillness and the emptiness in my life, when I stay with the solitude and the silence, that I can become aware of it. And yet "we are in the midst of it and it is in the midst of us, for it beats in our very blood, whether we want it to or not." This is something mysterious, and perhaps that is no bad thing for Merton is after all a poet and many truths can only be expressed through images whose full meaning I may not immediately grasp. So what does he mean by this cosmic dance? It is the universe, the cosmos as God made it, moving in perfect harmony with its Creator. It is a gift that God gave to Himself. "God made the world as a garden in which He himself took delight." He made man and woman in His own image. He also made them free. So we have this choice—to be separate and apart, succumbing to despair and sadness, or to discover our true identity, our real selves, which brings us joy and freedom, so that we shall then "be able to hear His call and follow Him in His mysterious, cosmic dance."

Perhaps this is nothing more than the "hidden wholeness" which I have tried to discover through pictures and words during this time of retreat. It is reflected uniquely in each created thing; it is inherent in each one of us; it is in some mysterious way the hidden wholeness of God Himself which binds together the persons and things of His creating.

> The heavens proclaim the glory of God
> and the firmament shows forth the work of His hands
> Day unto day takes up the story
> and night unto night makes known the message.
>
> No speech, no word, no voice is heard
> yet their span goes forth through all the earth,
> their words to the uttermost bounds of the world.

May the spoken words of my mouth,
the thoughts of my heart,
win favour in your sight,O Lord,
my rescuer, my rock!
(Psalm 18 [19], verses 1-4, 14)

Notes and References

How Do I Use This Time?

The first long quotation from Thomas Merton (on p. 18) is taken from *New Seeds of Contemplation* (New York: New Directions, 1962), pp. 82–83. There is a chapter on "Solitude" in *Seeds of Contemplation* (London: Hollis & Carter, 1949).

I have changed the word "men" which Merton used into "others" and this is something that I have done, where it seems appropriate and comes easily, throughout this book. I have also set out what he wrote in a form which I hope will encourage slow reading, staying with each phrase and allowing the full significance of the words to lead into prayer.

As a Trappist monk Merton would be living under the Rule of St Benedict, a rule that has guided the life of monks and nuns for 1500 years, since it was written in the sixth century, and increasing numbers of lay people are also finding that its good sense and practical wisdom can help them in their Christian discipleship today. There are many English translations, e.g., *RB 1980—The Rule of Saint Benedict 1980*, edited by Timothy Fry (Collegeville, MN: Liturgical Press, 1981).

The quotation from Merton's talk in California (on p. 21) is from David Steindl-Rast, who heard him there. It comes in a chapter on Merton "Man of Prayer" in *Thomas Merton/Monk: A Monastic Tribute*, edited by Br Patrick Hart (Kalamazoo, MI: Cistercian Publications, 1983), pp. 79–91.

The sentence about savouring and absorbing the psalms (pp. 21–22) I found when I was reading *Spiritual Direction and Meditation* (Collegeville, MN: Liturgical Press, 1960), p. 53.

The phrase in the following sentence (p. 22) comes in a letter to Fr Ronald Roloff OSB, February 14, 1964, *The School of Charity: The Letters of Thomas Merton on Religious Renewal and Spiritual Direction*, selected and edited by Br Patrick Hart (New York: Farrar, Straus and Giroux, 1990), p. 202. These letters make wonderful reading, full of wisdom and humour and much that is profound is said extremely simply.

Bread in the Wilderness is an early book, published in 1953 (New York: New Directions), and as a paperback in 1971 (Collegeville, MN: Liturgical Press).

The quotation on p. 23 from Theophane the Recluse is in *Woods, Shore, Desert: A Notebook, May 1968*, with introduction and notes by Joel Weishaus (Santa Fe: Museum of New Mexico Press, 1982). This is a lovely short book which has photographs by Merton taken on his trip to California.

The sentence about pace (p. 23) is from *New Seeds of Contemplation*, p. 242.

What Merton is saying about the fullness of time (p. 23) is part of that talk in California which I have used above. It comes on p. 81 of the chapter by David Steindl-Rast.

Words and Pictures

The phrases in this section are taken from the following sources:

Zen and the Birds of Appetite (New York: New Directions, 1968), p. 141.

Conjectures of a Guilty Bystander (New York: Doubleday, 1966), p. 179.

New Seeds of Contemplation (Garden City, NY: Doubleday, 1966), p. 16.

Ibid., p. 25.

Letter to Sister A., May 21, 1953, *School of Charity*, p. 61.

New Seeds of Contemplation, p. 29.

Emblems of a Season of Fury, in *A Thomas Merton Reader*, edited by Thomas P. McDonnell (London: Lamp Press, 1989), p. 506.

New Seeds of Contemplation, p. 19.

The Sign of Jonas (New York: Harcourt, Brace, 1953), p. 238.

Thomas Merton's Journey

Much of what I say here is based on Merton's autobiography *The Seven Storey Mountain* (New York: Harcourt, Brace, 1948). Since then there have been a great many editions including the English edition *Elected Silence* (London: Hollis & Carter, 1949). This was edited by Evelyn Waugh who wrote the introduction, and who shortened it considerably, reducing it by twenty per cent. While in many ways this is an improvement since he cut out much that was repetitious and made it much tauter, it *is* a different book, as Michael Mott says in his biography *The Seven Mountains of Thomas Merton* (Boston: Houghton Mifflin, 1984, p. 248): "It lacks the flavour of the original." In 1975 Sheldon Press produced the complete and unedited version.

For those who do not yet know Thomas Merton I would suggest that the best book with which to begin is *Living with Wisdom: A Life of Thomas Merton* by Jim Forest (Maryknoll, NY: Orbis Books, 1991). It is clear and concise, and full of photographs which are almost as valuable as the text.

The quotation about solitude on p. 33 comes from *The Sign of Jonas* (New York: Harcourt, Brace, 1953), p. 228. This is his journal of his early years at the monastery as, like Jonah of the title of the book, he finds himself brought to exactly the place where God wanted him to be.

The two following quotations (pp. 33–34) are also from *The Sign of Jonas*. The second one, where he speaks of the sacrament of the present moment, is dated January 18, 1950, and was written therefore well before his hermitage years. But I felt that I could include it here since it seems to catch the essence of a life lived so fully and completely in the present.

His journey to the East can be followed in *The Asian Journal of Thomas Merton* (New York: New Directions, 1968). This was edited from his notebooks by Naomi Burton, Patrick Hart and James Laughlin, and it is illustrated from his photographs. His address to the conference can be found on p. 337.

The sentence which begins "Our real journey in life is interior" (p. 35) I found in one of Merton's circular letters, published in the *Sewannee Review* LXXVII (1969): pp. 555–56. I owe this reference to Sr Agnes Hoomann RSCJ, "Our Real Journey in Life: A Study of Thomas Merton," *Review for Religious*, vol. 35 (1976).

I owe the extract about the journey without maps (p. 35) to Br Ramon's book *Soul Friends: A Journey with Thomas Merton* (Basingstoke: Marshall Pickering, 1989). See p. 125 for the full reference. This is another book that I would highly recommend to anyone who wants to discover more about Merton. I have changed "he" into "us" in this passage to allow us all to identify with it more easily—a liberty which I hope Merton would forgive.

The successive editions and translations of his books gave Merton the opportunity to write new prefaces. A number of these have been published under the title *Introductions East and West: The Foreign Prefaces of Thomas Merton*, edited by Robert E. Daggy (New York: Crossroad, 1989).

The quotation I use on pp. 35–36 is to be found on p. 129, of the above.

For the quotation that immediately follows (about answers, p. 36) see *Conjectures of a Guilty Bystander*, p. 38.

The sentences about simplicity (p. 36) come in a letter to Fr Kilean McDonnell, June 8, 1958, *School of Charity*, p. 111.

The tribute from a fellow-monk is from Matthew Kelty, who contributed a chapter called "The Man" to the volume *Thomas Merton/ Monk: A Monastic Tribute*, pp. 19–35. It is a charming portrait which opens "You could tell Father Louis by his walk." The part that I quote is on p. 27.

The letter that I refer to later in that same paragraph was to Dom Gabriel Sortais, March 1952, *School of Charity*, p. 36.

The Benedictine monk to whom Merton was writing (p. 37) was Fr Ronald Roloff OSB of Saint John's, Collegeville, Minnesota, September 26, 1962, and the letter is published in this same collection.

On p. 38 the reference is to *The Christmas Sermons of Blessed Guerric of Igny: An Essay by Thomas Merton,* sermons translated by Sister Rose of Lima (Abbey of Gethsemani, 1959), p. 25.

What Merton says about the way in which his father saw the world (pp. 39–40) comes very early on in his autobiography, *The Seven Storey Mountain*, p. 9, *Elected Silence*, p. 33.

Page 40 refers to *A Hidden Wholeness: The Visual World of Thomas Merton*, photographs by Thomas Merton and John Howard Griffin, text by John Howard Griffin (Boston: Houghton Mifflin, 1979).

The small phrase about the "observed particulars" (p. 41) comes from the catalogue of an exhibition of the work of David Jones the Welsh poet and artist, and it has stayed with me ever since because it catches the way in which a poet, the artist or the contemplative see the world.

Day One—The Call

The prayer of Merton's at the start of this day (pp. 45–46) I found included in the anthology *Pax Christi* (Erie, PA: Benet Press).

The psalms that I use are taken from the Grail translation. I have found that this presents them in a form that makes them easy to pray with.

What Merton says about contemplation (pp. 47–48) is taken from the first chapter of *New Seeds of Contemplation*, although, as with much of the material that I use, it is set out by me.

The paragraph which opens "In technology you have this horizontal progress . . ." (pp. 48–49) comes from something that I have referred to before, Merton talking in California on his last journey before he went to the East in 1968, and so it tells us what he was thinking towards the end of his life. It is to be found in David Steindl-Rast's chapter "Man of Prayer" in *Thomas Merton/Monk: A Monastic Tribute*, p. 80. I am aware that I have already quoted the end of this passage on p. 21 in the introductory section. If I repeat it here it is because I feel that it has something to say of the very greatest significance at the start of this retreat.

The sentence "It is true that our love for God . . ." (p. 50) comes in a letter that Merton wrote to Dom Gabriel Sortais on February 12, 1953, which seemed to me to say something so profoundly important that I have changed it into the form of a prayer. *School of Charity*, p. 52.

Describing his need for solitude as being like that of a plant needing the sun was part of a conversation that he had with Dan Walsh one day in September 1939 when he was still at Columbia. He tells us in *The Seven Storey Mountain* how they sat in the corner of the bar and talked about his vocation and the direction that his life should take.

"Solitude is not found . . ." (p. 51) was written on January 3, 1950, *The Sign of Jonas*, p. 255.

The following quotations on p. 51 come from "Notes for a Philosophy of Solitude" in *The Power and Meaning of Love* (Sheldon Press, 1976), p. 72, and the longer quotation on pp. 51–52 comes from *Contemplation in a World of Action* (Garden City, NY: Doubleday, 1971), pp. 218–25.

For what Merton has to say on the Desert Fathers see his *Wisdom of the Desert: Sayings from the Desert Fathers of the Fourth Century* (New York: New Directions, 1960).

Pages 53–54 quote John Howard Griffin, *The Hermitage Journals: A Diary Kept while Working on the Biography of Thomas Merton*, edited by Conger Beasley Jr. (Kansas City, MO: Andrews and McNeel, 1981), pp. 56–57.

"Keep still, and let Him do some work" (p. 54), *New Seeds of Contemplation*, p. 161.

Again I have found what Merton is saying in a letter is something that can be read slowly, almost as a prose poem, with attention and with prayer (pp. 55–56). These lines were written to the Indian poet, scholar and philosopher Amiya Chakravarty in April 1967. They come from another collection of letters, *The Hidden Ground of Love: The Letters of Thomas Merton on Religious Experience and Social Concerns*, selected and edited by William H. Shannon (New York: Farrar, Straus and Giroux, 1985), pp. 113–14.

Day Two—Response

The opening quotations (p. 59) are taken from a letter to Fr Bruno Scott James, October 1, 1960, *School of Charity*, p. 137.

"It takes courage . . ." (p. 60), *Conjectures of a Guilty Bystander*, p. 147.

"Let me be content . . ." (p. 60), *The Sign of Jonas*, p. 18.

After Psalm 64 [65] (p. 61), I have quoted from *Bread in the Wilderness*, p. 106.

Merton tells us of that episode with John Paul (pp. 62–63) in *The Seven Storey Mountain*, p. 9 (English edition, p. 23; *Elected Silence*, p. 22).

For the comment on the prodigal son (p. 63) see *Spiritual Direction and Meditation*, pp. 71–72.

The ideas on compunction were stimulated by reading what Merton said to the novices whom he was teaching at Gethsemani in 1951 but they are expressed in my words. He was very insistent that compunction was essential to the monastic and contemplative spirit. If I dwell on it here it is because I also find it something that helps me.

What Merton has to say on sorrow for sin (p. 65) again comes from a letter, this time to Fr Bruno Scott James, October 1, 1960, *School of Charity*, p. 138.

The two passages on the psalms (pp. 65–67) are taken from *Bread in the Wilderness*, pp. 61–64. The discussion in between on forgiveness (p. 66) comes from the section on "Monastic Peace" in *The Monastic Journey*, edited by Br Patrick Hart (Collegeville,

MN: Cistercian Publications, 1992, p. 72). See also an article, John Albert, "The Christ of Thomas Merton's Monastic Peace," *Cistercian Studies* XXIV, 3 (1989): pp. 264–74.

Day Three—
The Solitary Within:
The True Self

The opening sentence (p. 69) is taken from *Wisdom of the Desert* where Merton is speaking of the spiritual journey of the early Desert Fathers.

The quotation that follows (p. 69) comes from *New Seeds of Contemplation*, p. 26. The phrase that I use, "pilgrimage of identity," I owe to Br Ramon SSF, *Soul Friends: A Journey with Thomas Merton*. He has one chapter called "The Quest for Identity" which is an excellent introduction to Merton's thought on this subject.

"God leaves me to be free . . ." (pp. 70–71), *New Seeds of Contemplation*, p. 31.

"Free by nature . . ." (p. 71) is actually the second sentence of his autobiography, *The Seven Storey Mountain* (English edition, *Elected Silence*).

"If I never become . . . ," (p. 71), *New Seeds of Contemplation*, p. 26.

"There is an irreducible opposition . . ." (p. 72), *New Seeds of Contemplation*, p. 5.

"I must return to Paradise . . ." (p. 74); see "The Inner Experience: Christian Contemplation," *Cistercian Studies* XVIII (1983): p. 202.

The phrases "the smoke self," "the evanescent self" (p. 74) come in *New Seeds of Contemplation*, p. 33.

The first quotation in the paragraph which follows the psalm (p. 75) comes from a tape "Obstacles to Union with God," and the second from *Thoughts in Solitude* (New York: Farrar, Straus & Cudahy, 1958), pp. 52–53. Both are taken from James Finley, *Merton's Place of Nowhere: A Search for God through Awareness of the True Self* (Notre Dame, IN: Ave Maria Press, 1978), p. 72. Finley was for six years a novice at Gethsemani and was taught by Thomas Merton, which makes his book an invaluable introduction to Merton's thought.

In the following section I must acknowledge a debt to the chapter "Union with God" in John J. Higgins, *Merton's Theology of Prayer*, Cistercian Studies Series 18 (Spencer, MA: Cistercian Publications, 1971).

The long passage on p. 76 which opens "Souls are like wax . . ." comes in *New Seeds of Contemplation*, p. 161. I felt that the image came across particularly powerfully when it was set out in the form of a prose poem.

What Merton has to say on the second Adam can be followed further in *Disputed Questions* (New York: Farrar, Straus, 1953), p. 207.

Day Four—
Encounter with Christ

This first statement (p. 79) was one that Merton himself made in 1963 for the dedication of the Thomas Merton Studies Center at Bellarmine College. It is quoted by George Kilcourse, "Pieces of the Mosaic, Earth: Thomas Merton and the Christ," *The Message of Thomas Merton*, edited by Br Patrick Hart (Kalamazoo, MI: Cistercian Publications, 1981), p. 129.

The Dan Walsh quotation (pp. 79–80) comes from the same source, p. 132.

Merton mentions the mosaics in Rome over and over again in his writing, trying to define what they have meant to him. See *The Seven Storey Mountain*, pp. 108–11, or *Elected Silence*, pp. 95–98. For further references see footnote 85 on p. 584 of Michael Mott's biography, *Seven Mountains of Thomas Merton*.

"He is the whole meaning . . ." (pp. 80–81) is taken from Merton, *Basic Principles of Monastic Spirituality* (Trappist, KY: Abbey of Gethsemani, 1957).

Pages 81–82: *The Sign of Jonas*, p. 265.

"Christ has granted us His Friendship . . ." (p. 82) comes from *New Seeds of Contemplation*, pp. 153–54, and "Without Christ there would be no salvation . . ." (pp. 82–83) from *Basic Principles of Monastic Spirituality*. Perhaps I ought to say that with the latter where the original text reads "man" I have changed it in order to make it more personal, and so that it would be easier to use for prayerful reflection.

The meditation on the power of Christ on p. 83 is taken from "The Inner Experience: Christian Contemplation," *Cistercian Studies* XVIII (1983): p. 202. Here I have added daughters!

Page 84: *Christmas Sermons of Blessed Guerric of Igny,* pp. 2 and 44–46.

Merton quotes this sermon of Isaac of Stella (p. 85) in his *Silence in Heaven* (London: Thames and Hudson, 1956), p. 30. On its title page it is described as a book of the monastic life with ninety photographs and accompanying texts from religious writings.

The letter to Daisetz Suzuki is dated April 11, 1959, *The Hidden Ground of Love*, p. 564.

The passage that opens "This is the very root of our being . . ." (p. 86) is quoted by John Higgins, *Thomas Merton on Prayer* (New York: Doubleday, 1975), p. 40, but he gives no further reference.

What Merton says about "le point vierge" (p. 86) is from *Conjectures of a Guilty Bystander*, p. 143.

Day Five—
The Demands of Love

Many of the passages in this section originally read "brother" or "man" since Merton was writing out of his experience of living with and loving the brethren of his community. I have changed this in places where it seemed obvious but I hope that elsewhere anyone using this book will assume that they are not meant to be excluded.

"If I allow Christ . . ." (p. 89) comes from "The Power and Meaning of Love" in *Disputed Questions* (New York: Farrar, Straus, and Cudahy, 1960), pp. 97–127.

The following quotation (p. 90) I owe to Br Ramon where it comes on p. 122 of *Soul Friends*. He gives the reference as *Emblems of a Season of Fury* (New York: New Directions, 1963), p. 78.

I got the idea of the image of people in a circle (p. 90) from James Finley's *Merton's Place of Nowhere*, pp. 64–65.

Merton's discussion about illusions in loving (p. 91) is to be found in *Conjectures of a Guilty Bystander*, p. 131.

"If we believe in the Incarnation . . ." (p. 91) is taken from *New Seeds of Contemplation*, p. 229.

The quotation on pp. 92–93 which opens "A person is a person . . ." comes from *No Man Is an Island* (New York: Harcourt, Brace, 1955), pp. 244–45.

Pages 93–94: Merton describes what happened to him in Louisville in *Conjectures of a Guilty Bystander*, pp. 141–42.

Day Six—
*"Common and Natural
and Ordinary"*

The first paragraph (pp. 99–100) contains phrases taken from the opening page of *Seeds of Contemplation.*

The description of the bower in which Merton tells us he sat in silence (p. 100) is taken from *The Sign of Jonas*, p. 257, and the following quotation from p. 211.

What Merton has to say about time (p. 101) continues to refer back to a chapter that I have quoted before, David Steindl-Rast's "Man of Prayer" in *Thomas Merton/Monk: A Monastic Tribute*, p. 81.

The hymns on p. 102 were sung at the Abbey of New Clairvaux, Vina, California, while I was staying there. The first is by Aurelius Clemens Prudentius, AD 405, the translation from Ryde Abbey.

Merton's account of the rituals of the hermitage (pp. 102–3) comes from *Day of a Stranger* and is included in *Thomas Merton Reader*, p. 435.

John Howard Griffin's account (pp. 103–4) is taken from *The Hermitage Journals*, p. 49.

Pages 104–5 quote Edward Deming Andrews and Faith Andrews, *Religion in Wood: A Book of Shaker Furniture* (Bloomington: Indiana University Press, 1966), pp. x–xi.

Page 105: Merton tells us how his father saw the world in the first pages of the autobiography. John Howard Griffin tells us how Merton saw the world in his prologue to *A Hidden Wholeness*, especially pp. 3–4, where at one point he says "he worked as a painter might . . . ."

The quotation which opens "As soon as we take them to ourselves . . ." (p. 106) is from Merton, *The Silent Life* (New York: Farrar, Straus, and Cudahy, 1957), pp. 26–28.

Day Seven—Integration

The sentences which open this section (p. 109) come in a letter to Fr Thomas Fidelis Smith, January 19, 1963, *School of Charity*, p. 177.

The phrase "We must contain all divided worlds in ourselves" (p. 110) is from *Conjectures of a Guilty Bystander*, p. 21.

On the yin-yang symbol see Merton's essay "A Study of Chuang Tzu" in *The Way of Chuang Tzu* (New York: New Directions, 1965), pp. 15–32.

The two short sentences quoted on p. 112 are from *Conjectures of a Guilty Bystander*, p. 10.

"It is in deep solitude . . ." (p. 112) is taken from *The Sign of Jonas*, p. 261.

What Merton is saying about love (pp. 112–13) is in *Contemplation in a World of Action*, pp. 145–46.

Merton's discussion about social activists and solitude comes from Jim Forest, "The Gift of Merton," *Commonweal* 89 (1969): p. 464.

I end the retreat (pp. 115–17) by using the final chapter of *New Seeds of Contemplation*, "The General Dance," autobiography.